Robert E. Lee
First Soldier of the Confederacy

Robert E. Lee
First Soldier
of the
Confederacy

Earle Rice Jr.

**MORGAN
REYNOLDS**
Publishing, Inc.

620 South Elm Street, Suite 223
Greensboro, North Carolina 27406
http://www.morganreynolds.com

Civil War Titles

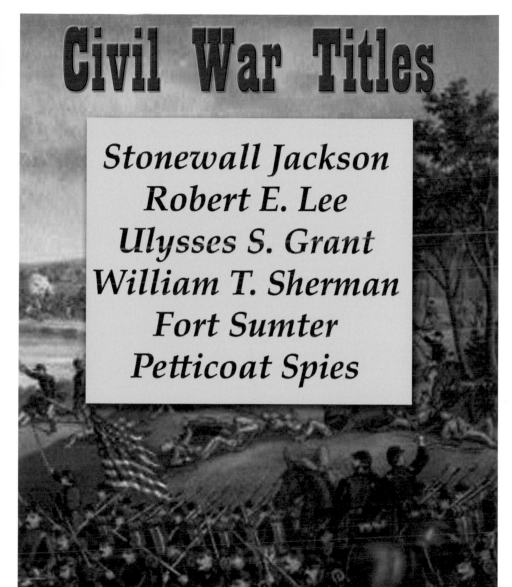

Stonewall Jackson
Robert E. Lee
Ulysses S. Grant
William T. Sherman
Fort Sumter
Petticoat Spies

ROBERT E. LEE: FIRST SOLDIER OF THE CONFEDERACY

Copyright © 2005 by Earle Rice Jr.

Rice, Earle.
    Robert E. Lee : first soldier of the Confederacy / Earle Rice, Jr.
        p. cm. — (Civil War leaders)
    Includes bibliographical references and index.
    ISBN 1-931798-47-8 (lib. bdg.)
    1. Lee, Robert E. (Robert Edward), 1807-1870—Juvenile literature. 2.
Generals—Confederate States of America—Biography—Juvenile literature. 3.
Confederate States of America. Army—Biography—Juvenile literature. 4.
United States—History—Civil War, 1861-1865—Campaigns—Juvenile
literature. I. Title. II. Series.
    E467.1.L4R53 2005
    973.7'3'092—dc22
                                                    2004021105

Printed in the United States of America
First Edition

Contents

1

Prospects

Robert E. Lee's father was one of the heroes of the American Revolution. Henry Lee's daring leadership and personal courage earned him a congressional medal and the nickname "Light-Horse Harry." (The cavalry distinguished between units based on the weight of the horses. Harry Lee's nickname derived from his cavalry command of "light" horses.) When General George Washington died in 1799, it was Harry Lee who made the famous tribute to his beloved commander. "First in war, first in peace, first in the hearts of his countrymen," declared Harry Lee, about the man he said he loved like a father.

In many ways, however, the Revolutionary War was the high point of Harry Lee's life. At its end, Light-Horse

Opposite: General Robert E. Lee *(Washington and Lee University Archives)*

Revolutionary War hero "Light-Horse Harry" Lee.

Harry's name and fame ranked second only to the reputation and renown of Washington himself. After he was honorably discharged from the Continental Army, Harry began what most thought was to be a long and brilliant period of public service. He served in Congress, under the Articles of Confederation, and as governor of Virginia for three one-year terms. While serving as governor, Harry met Ann Hill Carter, who grew up on the Shirley Plantation, a twenty-five thousand-acre estate in Charles City County, Virginia. Ann was the impressionable daughter of Charles Carter, one of the richest men in all Virginia.

Ann immediately succumbed to the charms of the dashing governor who, at age thirty-seven, was seventeen years her senior. Harry was a widower at this point and had a son from his first marriage. Ann and Harry married on June 18, 1793. They took their vows in the Great Hall of the Lee mansion, Stratford Hall, that stood— and still stands—on the north bank of the James River, about twenty-five miles southeast of Richmond.

Harry, however, had little money of his own. Even Stratford, where the couple was married, legally belonged to his son, who was also named Henry. It had been left to him by his mother who, before she died, had grown to dis-

Ann Carter Lee.

trust Harry's financial instincts. But at the time of the wedding of Harry and Ann, most people predicted a happy future for the couple. The Richmond *Virginia Gazette* even reported that the second Lee nuptials "promises the most auspicious fortune to the wedded pair" and "must give the highest satisfaction to their numerous and respectable relatives."

A friend and admirer of the bride found out differently soon after the wedding. Ann "became [Lee's] delighted wife, but to find in the short space of [two weeks] that her affections were trampled on by a heartless and depraved profligate," was how the friend put it.

Ann soon discovered that her new husband was an

impractical dreamer who was always looking for fortune around the next turn. He mismanaged his son's estate and dove impulsively into land speculations. Soon the couple was hopelessly, deeply in debt. Harry had to string chains across the steps at Stratford to try to keep the bill collectors out. In 1803, even Ann's father rewrote his will to put his daughter's inheritance in trust "free from the claim, demand, let, hindrance or molestation of her husband . . . or his creditors."

That same year, Ann became afflicted with edema—then called dropsy—an abnormal retention of fluid in body cavities or tissues caused by a disorder of the heart or kidneys. In letters to friends, she wrote of being "much of an invalid" and of "being much indisposed." The indignities of indebtedness and the increasing improprieties of her husband's speculations were taking a toll on her health.

By the time Ann became pregnant with her fifth child in 1806, Harry Lee had no financial credibility. The sheriff, acting on behalf of his creditors, knocked on their door regularly. Into this stressful environment Robert Edward Lee was born, at Stratford Hall on January 19, 1807. His father was delighted by another son; his mother worried about having another mouth to feed.

In April 1809, when Robert Edward Lee was two, his father's unpaid bills finally caught up with him. Light-Horse Harry Lee was arrested and sent to the county jail for indebtedness. While being jailed for debts did not carry with it the same degree of shame as did a criminal offense, it added yet another stain to Harry's already tarnished reputation. And Ann Carter Lee, whose father had raised her to treat money seriously, was humiliated. Harry tried to make the best of the situation. He used his time in confinement to begin writing his memoirs of his battle experiences.

After Harry had spent several months in the Westmoreland County jail and several more in the Spotsylvania Courthouse jail, a few of his relatives settled some of his more pressing debts and he was released from prison. When Harry returned home in the spring of 1810, he found that Henry, his surviving son from his first marriage, had completed his education at the College of William and Mary and, at the age of twenty-three, had returned to Stratford Hall to claim his birthright. Harry continued to work on his memoirs; the task of finding a new home fell to Ann.

While Harry was away, one of Ann's relatives had

The Lee family estate, Stratford Hall. *(Washington and Lee University Archives)*

invited her and the children to stay at his plantation, but she had politely declined, explaining that she had promised Harry she would remain at Stratford until he returned. But she reserved to herself the right to choose her next residence. Ann concluded, "I feel an unconquerable inclination to fix myself permanently, be it in ever so humble a manner, and must indulge myself, in at least making the attempt." Some time in the summer or fall of 1810, Ann, Harry, and their four children—Charles Carter (known as Carter), Sydney Smith (called Smith), Ann Kinloch, and Robert Edward—moved to Alexandria, the town of Ann's choosing.

According to an oft-repeated family tale, three-year-old Robert returned one last time to the southeast chamber at Stratford Hall where he was born to bid fond farewell to the two angels gracing the ironwork at the back of the fireplace.

The Marble Model

In Alexandria, then a town of 7,500, the Lees lived for a short while in a humble house at 611 Commerce Street, before moving to a more permanent residence at 607 Oronoco Street, a townhouse owned by William Henry Fitzhugh, Ann's third cousin. William, who lived in the country on his vast estate, Ravensworth, in Fairfax County, was happy to have Ann for a tenant. He thought of her as her "one of the finest women the State of Virginia ever produced."

The Fitzhughs' two-story brick house on Oronoco Street was tiny compared with Stratford Hall, but still quite elegant. Its location placed its new tenants squarely in the center of a community of relatives. Carter Lee later recalled "we had a large family circle" in Alexandria. The townhouse would be home to Robert for the next

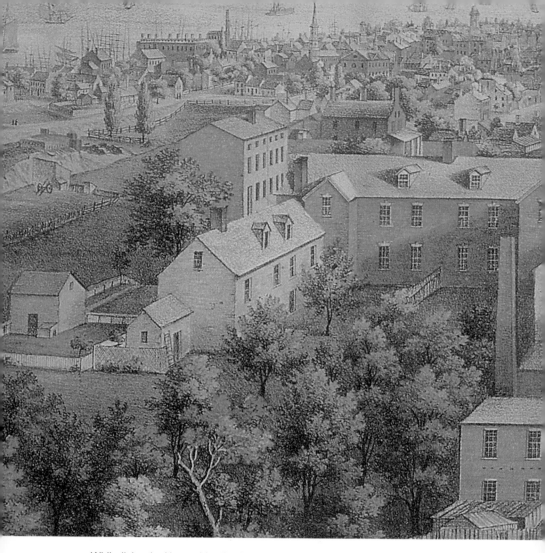

While living in Alexandria, the Lees occupied the two-story light-brick house in the foreground of this painting. *(Washington and Lee University Archives)*

fourteen years, and the town of Alexandria—as much as any other—deserves to be called his hometown.

Alexandria, which stands on the west bank of the Potomac River, six miles south of Washington, D.C., was a key port on the central Atlantic coast in the nineteenth century. Ships from all over the world tied up at its busy wharves to take on casks of tobacco from Virginia and Maryland. Its redbrick houses, cobblestone streets, street

lamps, numerous churches—and even a public library—
lent to Ann Carter Lee a sense of permanence and
prosperity that had eluded her for so long. The town also
supported thirty-four taverns, but people of fine breed-
ing rarely alluded to them in polite conversation.

One of the first things Ann did after arriving in
Alexandria was to give birth to Catherine Mildred (called
Mildred) Lee, her sixth and last child. With another
mouth to feed, Harry worked diligently to complete his
memoirs, hoping that profits from the sale of the book
would return him to solvency.

In the fall of 1811, Harry finally finished *Memoirs
of the War in the Southern Department of the United
States.* It appeared in print the following year. Although
the book presented a fairly accurate account of the
Revolutionary War campaigns, it did not sell well, and
Harry's dreams of recapturing lost fame and fortune
faded yet again. Perhaps the citizens of the new nation
had wearied of war by then. If so, they would soon find
cause to grow wearier yet.

On June 18, 1812, the U.S. Congress presented President James Madison with a declaration of war on Great
Britain. American grievances grew out of the oppressive
British maritime practices during the Napoleonic Wars.
Most egregious was the British practice of boarding U.S.
ships and forcing, or impressing, American sailors into
the British Navy.

About six weeks after war was declared, Light-Horse
Harry became a casualty of sorts. On July 28, while

visiting Baltimore, he was attacked by an angry mob for coming to the aid of a friend who had published antiwar newspaper editorials. Even as the drunken rioters clubbed and strangled him and beat him into the ground, Lee defied them and denounced them as "base villains." Horribly mangled and disfigured, the old warrior was given up for dead by attending doctors, but he somehow managed to survive and return to Alexandria in September.

Harry never fully recovered in Alexandria. In the autumn of 1813, with financial help from James Monroe and other sympathetic friends, Light-Horse Harry sailed for the Caribbean Sea. The old soldier hoped to speed his rehabilitation in a warmer clime, while at the same time foregoing fiscal responsibilities in favor of pursuing new fortune on the scattered islands of the West Indies. He promised his family to return fully recovered and to bring home riches commensurate with the lifestyle he thought they deserved. Robert was six years old when he watched his father board ship at Alexandria and sail off down the Potomac River. He would never see him again. Harry left behind a sullied reputation among many of his associates, but his family would always remember him as the dashing cavalryman of his glory days.

In two decades of marriage, Ann Carter Lee, who had grown up used to the pampering and comforts of great wealth, had matured into a strong-willed woman. It was she who held the family together, cared for the children, and supported the household. Ann received a sum of $1,200 annually, her inheritance from her father. The money, though less than a princely sum, provided her family with a comfortable home, and her children rarely lacked for necessities.

The following passage, which Ann wrote in 1816, offers an interesting glimpse of her careful menu planning, which was both frugal and satisfying:

> We have very seldom more than one dish on the table, of meat, to the great discomfort of my young Ladies and Gentlemen, whom you know have various tastes— It requires a length of time every night, to determine what shall be brought next morning from the market— As there is to be but one dish, all cannot be pleased: Ann [now sixteen] prefers fowls, but they are so high, that they are sparingly dealt in; and if brought to table, scarcely, a back, falls to Smith [now almost fourteen] and Robert's [now nine] share, so that they [would] rather not be tantalized with the sight of them; and generally urge the purchase of veal; while Mildred [now five] is as solicitous, that whortleberries or cherries should compose our dinner.

Carter is not mentioned because he had left home to attend Harvard University in Cambridge, Massachusetts. Harry wrote to him occasionally from the West Indies. His letters reflect a lonely man trying to pass on some of the wisdom he had acquired through years of his own misadventures. He never wrote directly to Robert, but in one missive to Carter he noted: "Robert was always good, and will be confirmed in his happy turn of mind by his ever-watchful and affectionate mother. Does he strengthen his native tendency?" Light-Horse Harry never received an answer to his question, but under Ann's loving guidance Robert's amiable nature and innate sense of responsibility did indeed grow stronger.

Details of Robert's early life are sketchy, and for the most part originate in family lore. His boyhood appears to have been unspectacular and much like that of any other active youth of his day. Ann's homeschooling provided him with the rudiments of reading and writing. She later sent him to a family school at the plantation home of her sister Elizabeth, one of two family schools operated by the Carters. When Robert returned home, he would occasionally misbehave. Ann complained to Elizabeth about it. Her sister told her that she had found Robert a charming child but she advised Ann to apply her own antidote for bad behavior: "Whip and pray, pray and whip." Elizabeth's prescription apparently worked, as no other reports of Robert's misconduct appear to exist.

Ann, a devout Christian, also taught Robert piety. He is said to have learned the Episcopal catechism before he could read. Ann held daily prayers with her family at home, and she attended the Christ Church of Alexandria—the church of George Washington—every Sunday with her children. According to one family member, Robert learned from his mother "to practice self-denial

Christ Church in Alexandria was not only the place of worship of Ann Carter Lee
and her children, but had also been the church of President George Washington.
(Library of Congress)

and self-control, as well as the strictest economy in all
financial concerns." He embraced these virtues, and
they served him well throughout his life.

Despite having an absentee father, Robert seemed to
have spent a happy boyhood. He enjoyed athletic activities such as riding, swimming, and hunting. After attending to his schooling and household responsibilities, he
could often be found with his friends flying kites, ice
skating, or chasing after mounted huntsmen and their
hounds in pursuit of foxes in the woods and meadows
of Virginia. He delighted in using little-known shortcuts

to race across the countryside and arrive at the quarry ahead of the hunters. In outfoxing the fox hunters, Robert demonstrated an early ability to anticipate the movements of others, a sense of terrain, and a flair for outrageous surprise—the essential elements of his generalship in later years.

Colonel Joseph Ives, an officer who later served on the staff of General Lee, bore witness to his leader's daring: "His name might be Audacity. He will take more desperate chances, and take them quicker than any other general in this country, North or South."

Robert grew strong, sturdy, and quite handsome, taking his nose from his father but his soft brown eyes from his mother. Growing up in Alexandria, where George Washington was idolized, Robert learned firsthand about his father's former commander. At an early age, he began to practice Washington's patience, courage, discipline, and self-control. Years later, he would say, "I cannot consent to place in the control of others one who cannot control himself." Perhaps the absence of self-restraint Robert witnessed in his own father caused him to value self-control as an essential virtue in himself and others.

The father whom Robert hardly knew died in 1818 when Robert was eleven years old. Harry, at age sixty-two, had finally conceded to himself that he was not going to recover his health. Wanting to die at home, he had set sail in early March from Nassau aboard a ship bound for Savannah, but he made it only as far as Cumberland Island, Georgia, where he was put ashore in great pain. Harry died on March 25, 1818, probably of cancer, at the Dungeness estate of his late Revolutionary comrade Nathanael Greene. He was buried with full military honors in the Greene family cemetery.

Ann Carter Lee, as faithful to her husband's memory as she had been to the man himself, made sure that Robert remembered his father as a hero and not as an idle dreamer and failed speculator be-

"Light-Horse Harry" Lee's tombstone on Cumberland Island, Georgia.

set by financial woes. Harry himself left only a legacy of advice in his letters to Carter, the sum of which amounts to "do as I say and not as I did." Robert read the letters, and some of Harry's words exerted a powerful influence over his life. "Self-command," wrote Harry, "is the pivot upon which the character, fame, and independence of us mortals hang." More poignantly, he warned, "Avoid debt, the sink of mental power and the subversion of independence."

In 1820, Smith Lee, with assistance from President James Monroe, received a midshipman's commission and left home to embark on a naval career. With his two older brothers gone, Robert, at age thirteen, suddenly became the man of the family. He dutifully handled many of the household chores, cared for the horses (with Harry gone, Ann could afford a carriage), and helped with the shopping and meal planning. His older sister Ann was sickly, and his younger sister Mildred was still too young to help. Robert did all he could to spare his mother from undue drudgery, for she was already exhibiting signs of the tuberculosis that would eventually kill her. When needed, he also spent a good deal of his time nursing his ailing mother and sister.

Often, when Ann felt well enough, Robert would accompany her on carriage rides to Ravensworth and elsewhere, just to get her out of the house and lift her spirits. He tended to his mother while other boys his age were out playing, and at a young age was an experienced nurse. Yet young Robert accepted his new responsibilities willingly and with never a sign of complaint. Quite simply, it was his duty to accept them; and duty—next to God—was already becoming the most important concept in his life. "Duty . . . is the sublimest word in our language," he would write many years later. "Do your duty in all things. . . . You cannot do more—you should never wish to do less."

Robert entered Alexandria Academy in 1820. Over the next few years, under William B. Leary, a learned Irishman and an excellent teacher, he studied the classics and excelled at mathematics. As he was completing the academy's curriculum, the time drew near for him to decide what he wanted to do with his life. Ann wanted him to follow a profession of some sort, but a cut in interest rates had reduced her inheritance by half. She could not afford to send Robert to Harvard as she had sent Carter. Since Smith had chosen a career as a naval officer, Ann hoped Robert might find a similar vocation—plus a four-year college education at government expense—in the army. Dutifully, he applied for admittance to the U.S. Military Academy at West Point, New York, in 1824.

As the son of a Revolutionary War hero, and with the support of a bevy of influential sponsors, Robert's acceptance at the academy was a virtual certainty. William Leary's recommendation of his former student was typical of many. He vouched for Robert's character and ability in this way: "In the various branches, to which his attention has been applied, I flatter myself that his information [learning] will be found adequate to the most sanguine [optimistic] expectations of his friends. With me he has read all the minor classics, in addition to Homer and Longinus, Tacitus and Cicero. He is well versed in arithmetic, Algebra, and Euclid [geometry]."

Robert received his appointment to the academy in March 1824, not long after his seventeenth birthday. Because of a surplus of successful candidates from Virginia, however, his entrance date—and that of his future friend Joseph E. Johnston—was put off until the summer of 1825. In the interim, to prepare himself for the rigorous curriculum that lay ahead at West Point, he enrolled in a newly opened private school. Robert impressed the school's owner, James Hallowell, with his thorough, meticulous approach to all his studies. "His specialty was *finishing up*," Hallowell wrote of Robert. "He imparted a finish and a neatness, as he proceeded, to everything he undertook." By the time Robert left home for West Point, he was well prepared—physically, mentally, and spiritually—to excel.

Robert's departure marked a sad day—another among many—for Ann Carter Lee. She had relied on her son for so much for so long. After he left, her health took a turn for the worse. Already frail at fifty-two, Ann's life force was ebbing fast, but she was determined to hold on until her children were well established on their own.

The U.S. Military Academy at West Point stands on a high plain on the west bank of the Hudson River, about forty miles north of New York City. It was established as a school of engineering on the strategic site of an old fort in 1802. Although situated in a majestic natural setting overlooking the river, the academy's array of physical structures posed a less attractive sight to the eyes of young Robert Edward Lee. At the time of his arrival, the academy consisted of four gray stone buildings, two of which were barracks. The third building housed a mess hall and the fourth building—a two-story, multipurpose structure—contained a chapel, a library, a laboratory, and classrooms.

The West Point curriculum offered an education in civil engineering that was unsurpassed anywhere in the

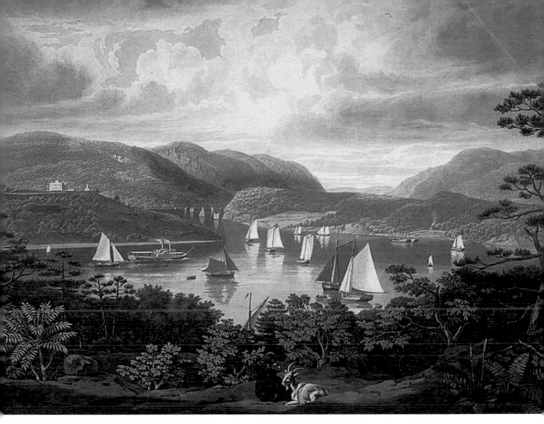

This view of West Point and the surrounding bluffs was painted not long after Lee arrived at the military academy. *(Library of Congress)*

country. Study encompassed the building of fortifications, the science of artillery, grand tactics, and military architecture. In the study of artillery, Robert and his fellow cadets learned about various types of guns and projectiles, along with range finding and ballistics. Grand tactics included military organization, the conduct of marches, battlefield formations, and the study of military maxims. (Tactics is the art of placing or maneuvering troops skillfully in battle; strategy is the planning and directing of the entire operation of a campaign or war.) And in the courses on military architecture, the cadets received instruction in civil engineering, mainly the construction of bridges, canals, and forts.

As the young cadet from Alexandria began his studies

and training at West Point, so also began the legend of Robert E. Lee. Never the best student in any given subject, he still managed to rank among the top five students in every class, which earned him a place on the distinguished lists. His extraordinary ability to adapt to the academy's routine and to perform his duties with uniform excellence set him apart. After completing his plebe (fourth-class or freshman) year, Cadet Lee was selected to serve as staff sergeant, the highest noncommissioned rank and honor available to a third classman (sophomore). He also served as acting assistant professor of mathematics, to lend a hand to fourth classmen who were grappling with their numbers.

During Cadet Lee's final two years, his academic courses grew increasingly more challenging, emphasizing advanced work on fortifications and readings on the science of war. As he began his first-class (senior) year, his overall commitment to excellence and natural leadership qualities earned him the highest rank a cadet can aspire to or achieve: the coveted rank of corps adjutant. Cadet Lee graduated second in his class of forty-nine in 1829 and was commissioned as a brevet second lieutenant in the Corps of Engineers.

What made Robert's accomplishments at the academy so remarkable was that he completed his entire four years without a single demerit, or black mark. His achievement was doubly remarkable in that he managed to keep his slate clean in an environment in which many of his peers coveted each demerit as a badge of honor.

By contrast, Robert believed rules and regulations were meant to be obeyed, and he obeyed them to the letter. More remarkably, he did so while still retaining the respect and admiration of his more rebellious classmates. He marched to his own drumbeat, and his peers accepted him for it. Many years later, Joseph E. Johnston, his classmate and fellow Virginian, explained what made his friend unique: "No other youth or man so united the qualities that win warm friendship and command high respect [as did Robert]. For he was full of sympathy and kindness, genial and fond of gay conversation, and even of fun, while his correctness of demeanor and attention to all duties . . . gave him a superiority that every one acknowledged in his heart."

Practically everyone who knew Lee shared Johnston's esteem and respect for him and for the intrinsic naturalness of his superiority that precluded envy in others. "I doubt if he ever excited envy in any man," wrote Erasmus D. Keyes, a lower classman and future Federal general. "All his accomplishments and alluring virtues appeared natural to him, and he was free from the anxiety, distrust, and awkwardness that attend a sense of inferiority."

Lee was twenty-two years old when he and his forty-eight classmates tossed their hats in the air at graduation. Fully grown at just under six feet tall, his square jaw, brown eyes, and wavy brown hair, set above broad shoulders and an erect, well-developed frame, combined to suggest the sculpted image of the quintessential soldier. To his classmates, Robert E. Lee was a model soldier lacking only a pedestal. They gave him a fitting nickname: the Marble Model. Yet seventeen years would elapse before Robert E. Lee would hear his first shot fired in anger and begin to fulfill the potential he had exhibited at West Point.

Test of a Soldier

Any jubilation Robert E. Lee may have felt over his graduation from the academy ended abruptly when he returned home to find his mother at Ravensworth in the final stages of her terminal illness. She had shown signs of improvement earlier that spring, but suffered a relapse. All Robert and others in attendance could do was to make her as comfortable as possible and pretend to be cheerful while waiting for the inevitable. Ann Carter Lee, who had wanted a permanent place of her own almost more than anything else in life, died as a houseguest of her third cousin, William Henry Fitzhugh, on July 26, 1829. Ann's death devastated Robert. Forty years later, he would stand at the doorway to the room where his mother had died and comment, "It seems now but yesterday."

As her legacy to her daughters, Ann Kinloch and Mildred, Ann Lee left her $20,000 trust fund, her personal effects, and a few house slaves to be equally divided between them. Ann Kinloch had married William Louis Marshall, a minister and later an attorney of note, in 1826. Mildred would marry Edward Vernon Childe, a wealthy Boston attorney, in 1831. To her three sons, Ann bequeathed a twenty thousand-acre tract of land in southeastern Virginia's Patrick County, and thirty slaves, at least some of whom were sold and the money equitably shared. The land came encumbered with unpaid taxes. The Lee legacy of debt would continue a while longer.

Brevet Second Lieutenant Lee, now without a place he could call home, spent the remainder of his graduation leave visiting his numerous relatives in Virginia. Among those he called on that summer was his childhood playmate and distant cousin, Mary Anne Randolph Custis. She was the daughter of Mary Lee Fitzhugh and George Washington Parke Custis. Her father was the grandson of Martha Washington by her first marriage, and the step-grandson and adopted son of the first president. The twisted branches of her family tree made Mary Anne the great-granddaughter of Martha Washington. Lee's visits to Arlington, the Custis family estate on the Potomac, suggest a romantic interest, but no evidence confirms that Lee courted young Mary at that time.

On August 11, 1829, Lee received orders to his first assignment, directing him "by the middle of November next [to] report to Major Samuel Babcock of the Corps of Engineers for duty at Cockspur Island, in the Savannah River, Georgia." He was to help construct a new fortification that would eventually bear the name of Fort Pulaski. If Lee had asked to be sent to the army's absolute worst duty station, Cockspur Island would not have disappointed him.

When Lee arrived at Cockspur in early November, it barely qualified as an island. Situated twelve miles downstream from Savannah, it consisted mainly of marshlands, most of which lay below sea level. Named for a nasty thorned plant, Cockspur Island was home to disease, an infinite variety of voracious insects—including the sand flea—and a brutal humidity that made work impossible in the summertime. For seventeen months, Lee spent the colder seasons applying and sharpening the skills he had learned at West Point, often immersed in muck and water up to his armpits. It was horrid duty but valuable training for the young engineer, and it was not without its compensations.

While at Cockspur, Lee became a frequent visitor to the Savannah home of the Mackays, the widowed mother and four sisters of Jack Mackay, his classmate and best friend at West Point. The Mackays welcomed young Lee, and he briefly courted two of the older sisters, Margaret and Eliza. Both girls chose different mates, but they would all remain lifelong friends. Apparently, he was determined to find a wife. During the summer work shutdown of 1830, Lee, at age twenty-three, proposed to

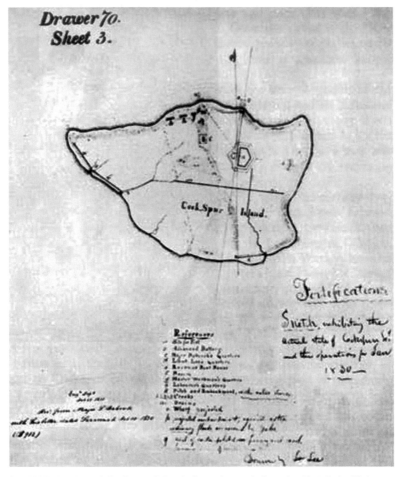

An 1830 drawing of Cockspur Island, Georgia, and plans for Fort Pulaski drawn by Lt. Robert E. Lee.

twenty-one-year-old Mary Custis, whom he affectionately called "Molly."

In a letter to his brother Carter on September 30, Lee wrote: "I am engaged to Miss Mary C. . . . That is, she & her mother have given their consent. But the Father has not yet made up his mind, though it is supposed [he] will not object." Mary's father initially did object. He felt

Robert's bride, Mary Custis Lee. *(Washington and Lee University Archives)*

that Lee could scarcely support his daughter on an army lieutenant's pay in the style to which she was accustomed. But George Washington Custis soon caved in to the pressure from his wife and daughter, and plans went ahead for a June wedding.

In April 1831, the army reassigned Lee to Fort (or Fortress) Monroe, overlooking Hampton Roads at the tip of Virginia's York Peninsula. He reported to his new duty station on May 7, 1831, to find that construction on the fort was nearing completion. His new duties would involve assisting Captain Andrew Talcott with the fort's outworks and the moat. Later, Lee would also direct the offshore construction of Fort Calhoun (later Fort Wool) on ripraps (stones sunk haphazardly in deep water to form a foundation). His transfer moved him much closer to Arlington and came at a most opportune time.

On June 30, 1831, Robert Edward Lee and Mary Anne Randolph Custis were married in a ceremony conducted at Arlington House by Reverend Reuel Keith, the Episcopal minister of Christ Church of Alexandria. Of Reverend Keith's service, Lee afterward remarked that he "had few words to say, though he dwelt upon them as if he had been reading my death warrant." Lee's marriage to Mary was hardly a death warrant, but it did represent one of the great turning points in his life. In the years to come, Mary would provide him with the things he wanted most in life—security, status, stability, and the

Robert and Mary were wed at Arlington House, the Custis family estate. Arlington House still stands, now as part of the Arlington National Cemetary outside of Washington, D.C.

Young Robert E. Lee, as painted by West Point professor Robert Weir.

tradition of a loving family. In return, he would provide her with deep and abiding love and devotion for the rest of his life.

An old adage insists that opposites attract. At the time of their marriage, Lee weighed about 170 pounds and stood just under six feet—tall for that time. He was startlingly handsome, robust, and vigorous, and maintained a soldierly bearing without conscious or apparent effort, moving with the grace and poise of an actor at ease in his role. Mary, like Ann Carter Lee, practiced her evangelical Protestant religion with zeal. She disapproved of Lee's "unchurched" status. Although some considered her attractive in her own way, she was less than ravishingly beautiful. Small and frail of figure, she would attract a variety of illnesses at a young age.

Lee patterned his life on order, neatness, and promptness; Mary slouched toward carelessness, neglect, and tardiness. Naturally reserved, Lee often kept his opinions to himself and treasured self-control; Mary was outspoken, quick to voice her views, and often acted impulsively. Despite their differences, Lee overlooked her flaws and gloried in her finer traits, always thinking about her best interests while ignoring his own wants; Mary returned his adoration and formed his conduit to family and faith. "Although she was never awed by his presence," noted one observer, "she had for his character a respect that became in time a positive reverence." This unlikely merger would last for almost forty years and produce seven offspring.

After a brief honeymoon at Ravensworth, Mary accompanied Lee to his new posting at Fort Monroe. There Mary discovered, to her chagrin, that her new home consisted of two rooms in a brick barrack. The rooms, which formed a wing of the quarters occupied by Lee's immediate superior, Captain Andrew Talcott, fell depressingly short of Arlington's comfort. Mary did not adapt well to army life or to the company of Lee's fellow officers and their wives, finding them "rather stupid."

Fort Monroe would later play an important role in the Civil War. This 1861 drawing of the fort shows the finished moat that Lee designed during his duty there in the 1830s. *(Library of Congress)*

When the Lees visited Arlington at Christmas, Mrs. Custis persuaded Lee to allow his now-pregnant spouse to remain there, where she would be more comfortable. Lee returned to Fort Monroe without Mary and spent the next few months alone. On May 17, 1832, the army removed the "brevet" (temporary) from his rank and his regular army ranking became effective on July 1, 1832, signifying the end of his initiation period. In the meantime, Mary, in response to Lee's letters urging her return, rejoined him in June. The reunited couple idled the summer months away, with Mary doing needlework while "Robert reads to me." Nevertheless, Mary's protracted stay at Arlington established a pattern of frequent long separations that was to become the rule rather than the exception over the next thirty years of their marriage.

In the peacetime army, officers and enlisted men more often than not sought relief from the humdrum of routine duties in card games or in drinking. Lee indulged in neither pastime. In a letter to a friend, Mary extolled Lee's "tender and affectionate" virtues and noted his preference for spending evenings at home "instead of frequenting the card games that attract so many." Except for an occasional glass of wine, Lee did not drink. A stickler for self-control, he distrusted the potentially adverse influence of hard drink. His abstinence from liquor set him apart from most of his peers.

As a classically handsome young army officer, Lee often turned the eye of a pretty young lady and enjoyed such attentions immensely. To his friend Jack Mackay, he once confessed his preference "in favor of the pretty girls if there are any here, and I know there are, for I have met them in no place, in no garb, in no situation that I did not feel my heart open to them, like the flower to the sun." Lee loved to flirt with the "pretty girls" in his life— Margaret and Eliza Mackay, Andrew Talcott's wife, Harriet, whom he called "my beautiful Talcott," and others—but he carefully avoided any kind of scandalous conduct. Even so, his flirtations have inspired speculation that his union with Mary was a loveless marriage, which he entered primarily to continue the Lee tradition of marrying well.

Lee's brother-in-law Edward V. Childe lent credence to such speculation when he observed that the Lee-Custis marriage, "in the eyes of the world, made Robert Lee the representative of the family of the founder of American history." It is true that Lee patterned himself after Washington and emulated him in his approach to duty and in his personal comportment. Moreover, Lee's marriage to the great man's great-granddaughter must have given him a sense of sharing in the heritage of the central hero of his life. It is also true that Mary—despite frequent separations—bore her husband seven children in thirteen years, which might suggest to some a marriage built on love.

Mary gave birth to their first child, a son named George Washington Custis Lee (called "Boo" or "Mr. Boo"), on September 16, 1832. Their first daughter, Mary Custis Lee ("the little woman"), arrived three years later in 1835. Next came another son, William Henry Fitzhugh Lee ("Rooney") in 1837, followed by daughters Ann Carter Lee ("Annie") in 1839, and Eleanor Agnes Lee ("Wigs") in 1841. Not until their first two sons drew their names from honored relatives would the Lees name their third son Robert Edward Lee Jr. ("Rob") when he arrived in 1843. Their fourth daughter and last child, Mildred Childe Lee ("Precious Life"), was born in 1846.

The physical demands of bearing seven children at a rate of one every other year took a toll on Mary's health. Always fragile, Mary contracted an abdominal infection after the birth of her first daughter in 1835 and remained bedridden for two months. A year later, she had the mumps, along with a fever. Lee wrote to Andrew Talcott, explaining that the fever "fell upon the brain, and seemed to overthrow her entire nervous system." Mary's early illnesses portended a future of debilitating

The two youngest Lee children, Mildred and Rob.

maladies. Rheumatism would afflict her in her mid-thirties and restrict her to a wheelchair in her mid-fifties. As a result of her nagging infirmity, Mary resided much of the time in the familiar environs of Arlington, where she raised her children in the absence of their father. Meanwhile, Lee, who was frustrated by long separations from his wife and family, and by a growing sense that his career was stagnating, had little choice but to seek escape in the performance of his duties.

In the summer of 1834, Brigadier General Charles Gratiot, chief of the Engineer Department, invited Lee to become his assistant in Washington, D.C. Lee had a few reservations about "the duties of the office" but accepted the general's offer. He assumed his new role in November 1834 at the age of twenty-seven. For the next twelve years, off and on into his thirty-ninth year, he would experience the tedium of mundane tasks and the dissatisfaction of painfully slow advancement. Lee was promoted to first lieutenant on September 21, 1836, seven years after graduating from West Point. He received his captaincy twenty-two months later on July 7, 1838. A further advance in rank would elude him for another nine years.

In the summer and early fall of 1835, Lee escaped from his desk-bound tedium in Washington when he helped to lay out the disputed boundary line between Ohio and Michigan. He described the country as savoring "marvelously of Bilious Fevers" and one that "seems to be productive of nothing more plentifully than of [mosquitoes] & Snakes."

While he traversed the wooded midlands, Mary, pregnant with Mary Custis and feeling unwell, implored him to return at once. He replied: "[W]hy do you . . . tempt [me] in the strongest manner, to endeavor to get excused from the performance of a duty, imposed upon me by my Profession, for the pure gratification of my private feelings?" Greatly underestimating the severity of his wife's ailments, he chose duty over personal needs. When he returned after finishing his assignment, he found Mary suffering from a pelvic infection, two abscesses of the groin, and the beginnings of her lifelong arthritis. She took several months to recover. For a time, Lee considered resigning his commission in order to be closer to his wife, but in the end decided he could not abandon his career.

In 1837, the army entrusted Lee with the most important independent job of his career up till then. The current of the Mississippi River was eroding the shoreline on the Illinois side and forming alluvial deposits in front of St. Louis, which threatened to transform the bustling river port into a stranded inland city. Lee left Arlington for St. Louis in June 1837, two weeks after the birth of his second son, William Henry Fitzhugh Lee. For the next four years, Lee oversaw the complex engineering and construction that kept the river navigable and assured the future of St. Louis as a port city.

The mayor of St. Louis noted that Lee worked "day by day in the hot broiling sun," sharing the "common fare and rations furnished to the common laborers . . . but never on any occasion becoming too familiar with the men. He maintained and preserved under all circumstances his dignity and gentlemanly bearing, winning and commanding the esteem, regard, and respect of every one under him." During that time, the Lees had two more daughters, Ann Carter in 1839 and Eleanor Agnes in 1841. Lee's work on the river earned him his captain's bars and later a transfer to Fort Hamilton in 1841, where he took charge of building fortifications in New York harbor.

Lee's career for the next five years proved far less

Mary Lee was said to have very much approved of the likeness of this 1838 portrait of her thirty-one-year-old husband. *(Washington and Lee University Archives)*

challenging than his work on the Mississippi. While headquartered at Fort Hamilton, his basic duties consisted of replacing rotten gun platforms and casements at four installations at the Narrows, between the Upper and Lower New York Bays—the strait now spanned by the Verrazano-Narrows Bridge. Although officially stationed in New York during this period, Lee also served as assistant to Colonel Joseph G. Totten, General Gratiot's successor as chief of the Engineer Department, and as a member of both the Board of Visitors to West Point and the Board of Engineers for Atlantic Coast Defense. These far-flung responsibilities required frequent travel and kept him busy.

Mary and the children eventually joined Lee at Fort Hamilton. While posted there, the Lees made one more addition to their family. After a little terrier Lee had saved from drowning delivered a litter of puppies, the children kept one and named him Spec. The dog became the only dog ever known to win Lee's affection. Spec even accompanied the family to church and sat with them during Sunday services. Lieutenant Henry J. Hunt, a fellow churchgoer, remarked that the Lee family "formed a charming portion of our little society."

One of the highlights of Lee's service in New York came in June 1844 when he served on the Board of Visitors to West Point for two weeks. One of his colleagues there was Major General Winfield Scott. Their job was to examine the first classmen (seniors) and to review the operation of the academy. Scott, a hero of the

This daguerrotype of Lee with his son Rooney was made in 1845.

War of 1812, had become the army's general in chief shortly after Lee's arrival at Fort Hamilton. An enormous man, Scott stood six feet five inches and weighed 230 pounds at age nineteen and continued to add poundage thereafter. His colorful complexion, dress, and language had earned him the nickname of "Old Fuss and Feathers." Scott and Lee, fellow Virginians, liked each other at once. Lee's judgment and intelligence deeply impressed Scott. Although Lee could not know it then, the

General Winfield Scott. *(Library of Congress)*

hulking general would soon become his greatest advocate in the army.

In 1845, the major topic of national discussion was the long-standing boundary dispute between the people of Mexico and the people of Texas. In June 1845, as the tension intensified, Lee informed his superior Colonel Totten, "In the event of war with any foreign government I should desire to be brought into active service in the field with as high a rank in the regular army as I could obtain. If that could not be accomplished without leaving the Corps of Engineers, I should then desire a transfer."

At age thirty-eight, Lee had served in the army for sixteen years, not counting his four years at West Point. At that point in his career, he was a highly skilled professional engineer and generally recognized by his superiors as one of the army's finest soldiers. But the true test of a soldier comes on the battlefield—and Captain Lee was about to be tested.

Lessons in the Art of War

On March 2, 1836, Texas declared its independence from Mexico and became the Republic of Texas. Mexico refused to recognize the new republic and Texans began a nine-year struggle for independence. In February 1845, the U.S. Congress passed a joint resolution to annex Texas. The resolution, subject to Texan approval, contained an amendment permitting Texas to be divided into five slaveholding states. In June, Texas accepted the resolution and was admitted to the Union on December 29, 1845, as the twenty-eighth state of the United States of America. Still, Mexico continued to claim Texas as its own. The stage was set for trouble.

In 1844, James K. Polk had been elected president on a platform promising to expand the U.S. John Tyler, Polk's predecessor, completed the annexation of Texas (pending the approval of Texans) during his last days in office. Polk was also determined to acquire Oregon, California, and New Mexico—by purchase if possible, by force if need be.

Soon after Polk took office, Mexico formally protested the annexation of Texas and broke off diplomatic relations with the United States. Polk sent an envoy to Mexico to resolve the Texas issue and to arrange the purchase of additional Mexican territories. Mexico rejected Polk's proposals, and the two nations moved toward war.

While still a republic, Texas had claimed the Rio Grande as its western boundary. The United States accepted that border at the time of annexation. Mexico, however, held that the true border lay along the Nueces River, 150 miles east of the Rio Grande. Texas had never exercised any authority over the intervening territory. On January 13, 1846, to ensure U.S. dominion over the disputed land—or, as some say, to provoke a war—Polk ordered a force under Brigadier General Zachary Taylor to take up position on the east side of the Rio Grande, opposite Matamoros, Mexico. Mexico considered Taylor's force to be encroaching on Mexican territory.

The inevitable clash occurred on April 25, 1846. Mexican troops from Matamoros crossed the Rio Grande north of Taylor's position and ambushed sixty-three American dragoons under Captain Seth Thornton, killing eleven and capturing most of the others. The next day, Taylor notified Washington that "hostilities may now be considered as commenced."

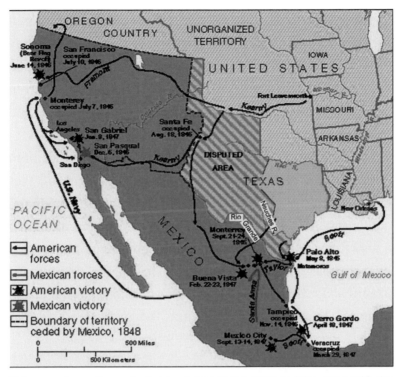

This map shows the contested territories of the Mexican War, along with the critical moves and battles of the opposing armies.

Two weeks passed before President Polk received Taylor's message. In the mid-1800s, communications took awhile. On May 11, Polk delivered a war message to Congress, stating, "After reiterated menaces, Mexico has passed the boundary of the United States, has invaded our territory and shed American blood upon the American soil." Congress passed a declaration of war the next day. By then, General Taylor and about twenty-three hundred regular army troops had already won two victories. A Mexican army of some six thousand troops under General Mariano Arista had attempted to cut

Taylor off from his supply line. The Americans battered the Mexicans with superior artillery at Palo Alto on May 8, and routed them the next day at Resaca de la Palma. On May 18, Taylor crossed the Rio Grande and entered Matamoros almost unopposed. The Mexican War had begun.

Neither nation was really prepared for a war, but both sides entered the conflict supremely confident of victory. Mexico's generals shared the general European contempt for American military prowess and anticipated a short war. President Polk, with a similar contempt for his adversary, saw the chance to fulfill the promise of Manifest Destiny—the claim of Americans to the right assigned to them by Providence "to overspread and to

After a day of difficult fighting at Palo Alto, Mexican general Arista withdrew to a more defensible position at Resaca de la Palma, a nearby dry riverbed (*resaca* means "dry riverbed" in Spanish), to wait for Taylor's troops. These well-laid plans were thwarted, however, by infighting among the Mexican officers, difficult communication, and a surprise attack on the Mexican flank. *(Library of Congress)*

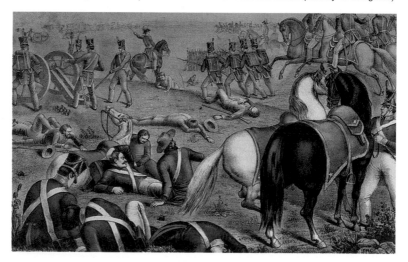

possess the whole of the continent." To this purpose, he sent additional forces under Colonel Stephen W. Kearny on a westward drive through the New Mexico Territory and on to California. Polk believed that Mexico would concede defeat if U.S. forces occupied the Rio Grande and captured key cities in New Mexico and California.

In the meantime, Captain Robert E. Lee continued to perform his routine duties at Fort Hamilton, watching the war pass him by and growing more restless with each passing day. He knew that advancement and the best assignments in the army—not to mention fame and glory—went to those officers who distinguished themselves in battle. In June 1846, Lee wrote to Jack Mackay: "I have been very anxious to join the army in Mexico, and had hoped to have joined Gen. Scott this fall at least." Lee's long-awaited orders finally arrived on August 19, posting him to a combat assignment with Brigadier General John E. Wool in San Antonio, Texas, where he reported on September 21.

The U.S. strategy now called for a joint attack in northern Mexico, with General Taylor moving south-westward against Monterrey from a staging (assembly) area at Camargo, while General Wool attacked westward against Chihuahua from San Antonio. This strategy would change several times over the next four months, during which time Lee performed the usual duties of a combat engineer in the field, including reconnaissance, road building, and bridge construction. He still had not heard the sound of hostile gunfire, but he was at least cam-

This picture of Lee was made during the early part of the Mexican War.

paigning with a fighting unit in enemy territory.

Christmas 1846 found Lee encamped at Saltillo, far from the warmth of home and family. In a letter to his wife Mary at Arlington, he wrote: "It is the first time we have been entirely separated at this holy time since our marriage. I hope it does not interfere with your happiness, surrounded as you are by father, mother, children, and dear friends. I therefore trust that you are well and happy, and that this is the last time I shall be absent from you during my life."

By the end of 1846, U.S. forces had achieved success in their opening campaigns on all fronts, from the Rio Grande to the Pacific Ocean, but their successes failed to bring the Mexican government to peace negotiations. President Polk now decided that the way to defeat Mexico was to launch a seaborne invasion of Veracruz and drive 264 miles inland to capture the Mexican capital of Mexico City. Winfield Scott, general in chief of the army and Polk's political rival, had advocated precisely such a strategy all along. Polk reluctantly assigned Scott to command the new campaign. Old Fuss and Feathers began preparing at once from a staging area in Brazos, Texas.

Polk authorized General Scott to draw troops as needed from General Taylor's forces in northern Mexico. On January 6, 1847, Scott wrote to Taylor from Brazos: "Of the officers of engineers, topographical engineers, and ordnance, with you, or under your command, I propose to take only Captain R. Lee, of the first named corps."

Lee set out from Saltillo on his fortieth birthday, January 19, 1847, and rode his bay mare Creole some 250 miles to join Scott's staff in Brazos. He reported to Colonel Joseph Totten, his old boss in Washington, D.C., who was now with Scott as his senior engineer officer. Lee, along with Totten, Lieutenant Colonel Ethan Allen Hitchcock, and Captain Henry Lee Scott, formed what Scott termed his "little cabinet," the inner circle of the general's advisors.

Beneath Scott's pompous, ostentatious exterior, he was a great general. Under his direction, Lee would learn invaluable lessons about the art of war. He would also render invaluable service to Scott in return. Jefferson Davis, the future president of the Confederacy, who served under Taylor in northern Mexico, would later write: "History will record, as Scott himself nobly admitted, that Lee was Scott's right arm in Mexico."

General Scott sailed with his staff to Tampico on

The American forces, under General Scott, landed near Veracruz on March 9, 1847. *(Library of Congress)*

February 15. Five days later, they continued down the eastern coast of Mexico for about fifty miles to Lobos Island, the staging area for his invasion fleet and forces. Lee bunked with his good friend Joe Johnston, of whom he wrote, "[M]y poor Joe is so sick all the time I can do nothing with him." Scott's invasion armada—about eighty ships carrying some twelve thousand American troops—set sail for Veracruz on March 2, and lead elements began arriving at Antón Lizardo, twelve miles below the target city, three days later. The entrance to Veracruz, a walled city protected by natural and man-made barriers, was guarded by a huge stone fortress on the island of San Juan de Ulúa. British naval officers swore that the 128-gun fort could "sink all the ships in the world."

Scott wisely decided to land his forces a few miles southeast of the city, beyond the range of Ulúa's guns. Scott sent Lee to reconnoiter the area. After an afternoon naval barrage, the invasion began at dusk on March 9, just as the sun touched the snowy peak of Mount Orizaba far to the west. By midnight, the Americans had invested (besieged) the walled city and had not lost a single man. On Lee's recommendation, Scott moved his heavier naval guns ashore to batter the city's walls. During the ensuing artillery bombardment, Scott virtually entrusted the siege of Veracruz to his engineers—Lee, Joseph E. Johnston, Pierre G. T. Beauregard, George B. McClellan, and others. On occasion, a young infantry lieutenant named Sam Grant accompanied them to observe their progress.

Day after day, the engineers went out to reconnoiter the city's defenses and terrain and to set up gun emplacements. On March 19, Lee experienced a near brush with death when rounding a turn in a path on his return from a work party. A surprised American soldier mistook him for one of the enemy and fired his pistol directly at Lee. The soldier's bullet singed Lee's uniform as it passed harmlessly between his left arm and his body.

On March 22, General Scott sent a surrender demand but the Mexicans refused to give up. Scott opened fire with land artillery and naval gunfire. Meanwhile, Lee was hard at work preparing his naval gun battery— three 32-pounders and three 8-inch shell guns—for action ashore. Scott ordered the battery to open fire at 10:00 AM on March 24, with Lee directing its fire.

Interestingly, on the occasion of Lee's baptism of fire, his brother Smith was among the naval officers assigned to the naval gun crews. Even though Robert was the younger of the two brothers, he apparently felt responsible for his older brother's safety. Lee later recalled the event: "No matter where I turned, my eyes reverted to him, and I stood by his gun whenever I was not wanted elsewhere. Oh! I felt awfully, and am at a loss what I should have done had he been cut down before me. I thank God that he was saved. He preserved his usual cheerfulness, and I could see his white teeth through all the smoke and din of the fire."

Lee had good cause to fear for his brother's safety. One day, four sailors, who were trained not to flinch at the flash of their guns at sea, stood erect at their guns and had the tops of their heads blown off. They had not learned that it was no disgrace to take cover from enemy fire on land.

After three days of intense bombardment, both the city of Veracruz and the fort at San Juan de Ulúa surrendered on March 27. Scott sent his victory dispatch back to Washington with Colonel Totten. In an order two days later, Scott included Lee among those who were "isolated by rank or position as well as by noble services." Upon Totten's departure, Lee became the second-ranking engineering officer in Scott's command. In the operations to come, however, Scott seemed to consult Lee much more than Major John L. Smith, the senior engi-

General Zachary Taylor. *(Library of Congress)*

neer, who was not well.

Scott had hoped that the fall of Veracruz would induce the Mexican government to sue for peace, but that did not happen. While Scott was occupied in the south of Mexico, General Zachary Taylor had defeated an army under General Antonio López de Santa Anna at Buena Vista, near Saltillo, in a two-day battle (February 22–23). After his defeat, Santa Anna retreated to Mexico City, assumed the presidency of Mexico, and prepared to defend the capital city with an army upwards of twenty thousand men. He developed a plan to inflict high casualties on the Americans by positioning defenses at towns and mountain passes along the main route to Mexico City. Scott, eager to leave Veracruz before the start of the yellow fever—or *vómito*—season, began his march to the city on April 8. He chose Jalapa, a city in the highlands on Mexico's old National Road, about seventy-four miles inland, as his first target.

On the advance inland, Lee accompanied Brigadier

General David E. Twiggs's division. The Americans encountered the enemy in force for the first time at Cerro Gordo, or Big Hill. Santa Anna's forces numbered about six thousand strong and blocked the approach to Jalapa, twenty miles to the west. Scott arrived at the site on April 14. After Lieutenant P. G. T. Beauregard, of the engineer corps, reported he had found a possible way around the enemy force, Scott ordered Lee to make a further reconnaissance the next morning.

While making his way through heavy underbrush the next day, Lee stumbled on a group of Mexican soldiers at a spring used as a watering hole. Before they saw him, Lee hit the ground and slowly crawled behind a nearby log. He lay there all day under a blazing sun, scarcely breathing and beset by voracious insects. Enemy soldiers came to fill their canteens and even sat on the log and chatted before going on their way. Lee kept still as the log that he lay behind until nightfall. Under a veil of darkness, he hurried back to the American camp and reported to Scott that he had found a trail that led around to the left of the Mexicans.

On April 17, Lee led Twiggs's division around the Mexican defenders, and Scott's army routed Santa Anna's army the next day in what became known as the battle of Cerro Gordo. The Mexicans fled so hurriedly that Santa Anna left his baggage wagon behind. Inside it, the victors found his military chest containing coin to pay his soldiers, some cooked chicken, and—best of all—Santa Anna's spare wooden leg. In his report of the

This painting depicts the fleeing Mexican forces at the battle of Cerro Gordo and the discovery of Santa Anna's wooden leg, among other things, in the baggage wagon that was left behind. *(Library of Congress)*

battle, Scott wrote: "I am impelled to make special mention of the services of Captain R. E. Lee, engineers. This officer, greatly distinguished in the siege of Vera Cruz, was again indefatigable . . . in reconnaissance as daring as laborious, and of the greatest value. Nor was he less conspicuous in placing batteries, and in conducting columns to their stations under the heavy fire of the enemy."

On May 15, 1847, Scott paused at Puebla, a town about seventy-five miles from Mexico City, to await fresh troops from the United States. With a force of almost eleven thousand men, he resumed his advance to the beat of drums and the blare of bugles on August 7.

A screen of lakes and marshes guarded the approaches to the Mexican capital. On August 18, Scott again called on his engineers to find a viable path to his objective.

Once again, Lee distinguished himself, this time finding a route through the Pedregal, a morass of lava-strewn stones some ten square miles in area. His skill at path finding and positioning of artillery and infantry largely accounted for Scott's victories at Contreras and Churubusco, south of the city. Lee's repeated trips across the wilderness of unfamiliar stone blocks and treacherous lava fissures in a torrential rain, and his advances with the infantry under fire, again earned the praise of Scott. The flamboyant general reported that "the gallant, indefatigable Captain Lee" had executed "the greatest feat of physical and moral courage . . . by any individual in my knowledge." And Lee was not done yet.

On September 11, Scott held a council of war a few miles south of Mexico City and decided on the castle of Chapultepec as his next objective. The castle, home of Mexico's National Military Academy, stood on a rocky, walled hill of the same name, two hundred feet above the plain. Artillery was needed to soften the defenses of the fortress for an infantry attack. Scott placed Lee in charge of positioning the gun batteries. Lee worked without sleep to position three gun batteries for the bombardment of Chapultepec, which began at dawn on September 13.

At 8:00 AM, the artillery barrage lifted and the U.S. 3rd and 4th Infantry Divisions, led by Generals Gideon Pillow and John Quitman, respectively, scaled the heights of Chapultepec and overran the castle by 9:30 AM. Lee joined Pillow's division in a rush across the plain and through a grove of cypress trees. Pillow was wounded and Lee escorted him to safety. After the fall of the fortress, Lee rode to the scene with Scott amid the cheers of the soldiers. Scott then sent Lee to reconnoiter the San Cosme Gate to Mexico City. Sometime during the afternoon, Lee incurred a minor wound that cost him a little blood. By the time he reported back to Scott, he had not slept in fifty-six hours. Exhausted and weakened by loss of blood, Lee, as he wrote later, "could no longer keep my saddle." But his efforts paid off.

Mexico City fell to Scott's army on September 14. The war with Mexico officially ended with the signing of the Treaty of Guadalupe Hidalgo on February 2, 1848. The Mexican War claimed the lives of over thirteen thousand Americans. It was a war that served as a training ground for some of the best officers in the world, and not least

In one of the last battles of the war, American forces charge the castle at Chapultepec. *(Library of Congress)*

among them was Robert E. Lee.

Lee earned three brevet promotions for heroism—at Cerro Gordo, the Pedregal, and Chapultepec. He emerged from the war with the rank of brevet colonel. (Brevet promotions were awarded in place of medals at that time.) General Winfield Scott called him "the very best soldier I ever saw in the field." Scott, according to Erasmus D. Keyes, a future Federal general who knew him well, had an "almost idolatrous fancy for Lee, whose military ability he estimated far beyond that of any other officer of the army." In a letter to Mary, Lee showed evidence of his maturation as an officer: "Fighting is the easiest part of a Soldier's duty. It is the watching, labouring, starving, freezing, willing exposure & privation that is so wearing to the body & trying to the mind. It is in this state that discipline tells, & attention night & day on the part of the Officer so necessary. His eye & thoughts must be continually on his men."

Lee had come to Mexico as a fine engineer; he would leave as a soldier of the first order, no longer relegated to the shadow of his father's valorous performances on the battlefield.

Lee learned many valuable lessons in Mexico, but two stand out in importance: First, he learned confidence in his own ability to command and to accomplish what had to be accomplished. Second, as a member of Scott's inner circle, he learned that a small army can defeat a much larger one by decisive action and skillful maneuvering. Scott taught Lee to take calculated risks based on accurate reconnaissance and careful analysis, and to act decisively even when his decision might fly in the face of conventional wisdom or the majority opinion of subordinates. Lee also learned to favor the philosophy of attack and to shun defense. As history reveals, his last lesson would sometimes undermine the best interests of his cause.

Colonel Lee returned home on June 29, 1848. He had been away for almost two years. When he rode up the long hill to Arlington, only his dog Spec recognized him.

5

Lee's Choice

Twenty-one months in Mexico had touched Robert E. Lee's hair with gray and scribed his face with furrows. When he returned home his family did not recognize him at first, and he mistook another boy for his youngest son, Rob, whom he had never seen. But he returned a hero, esteemed for his accomplishments by his superiors and his family and friends. Jefferson Davis would later comment, "He came from Mexico crowned with honors, covered with brevets, and recognized, young as he was, as one of the ablest of his country's soldiers." The fame he had earned during the Mexican War in 1847 was only the beginning of his renown. For the next fourteen years, however, he would again find himself consigned to a succession of routine postings, long separations from family, and slow advancement.

Soon after Lee's return, Engineer Chief Joseph G. Totten, now a brigadier general, temporarily assigned him to his office in Washington, D.C., while Lee completed work on various maps he had begun in Mexico. While working in the capital, Lee lived across the river at Arlington, where, as he wrote his brother Smith, he was "perfectly surrounded by Mary and her precious children." In the autumn of 1849, Totten reassigned Lee to Baltimore to supervise the construction of Fort Carroll. Lee spent the next three years in the city at the upper end of the Chesapeake Bay, forty miles northeast of Washington. Mary divided her time between the redbrick row house Lee rented in Baltimore and their home in Arlington.

Perhaps the most significant thing to happen to Lee during his three years in Baltimore came as an epiphany— a sudden, illuminating experience—while attending church. He had been raised in a religious setting and by most standards was already a good Christian, someone who always did his best to live a good life. Even so, Mary, who was devoutly pious, worried about him and prayed for his conversion. One Sunday, Lee heard a sermon that had a powerful impact upon him. At long last, in his early forties, he seems to have suddenly understood the dogma of original sin, which caused him to view himself as a flagrant sinner. "Man's nature is so Selfish, so weak," he wrote Mary. "Every feeling, every passion urging him to folly, excess & sin that I am disgusted with myself & sometimes with all the world." His newfound religious awareness would thereafter form an essential part of his character. Lee, along with his daughters Mary and Annie, would later be confirmed in the Episcopal faith at Christ Church in Alexandria by the bishop of Virginia, John Johns, on July 17, 1853. Mary would thereafter rest easier.

Early in 1850, Lee secured an appointment to West Point for his oldest son, Custis, who became a plebe in July of the same year. Almost two years later, on May 28, 1852, Lee received a letter from General Totten, appointing him superintendent of the military academy and commander of the post of West Point. Lee recognized the honor attached to the assignment but accepted it with great reluctance, noting, "I learn with much regret the determination of the Secretary of War to assign me to that duty, and I fear I cannot realize his expectations in the management of an Institution requiring more skill and more experience than I command." Lee's request that

Custis Lee.

another successor be assigned to the post was denied. The Lees reported to the academy on the Hudson on September 1, 1852, and Lee undertook his role as the academy's ninth superintendent.

Always an active man, Lee would have much preferred an assignment in the field, but, as he had advised Custis earlier, he accepted things as they were. "Take them as you find them," he had written his son. "Make the best of them. Turn them to your advantage." In two and a half years at West Point, he oversaw significant changes in the school's curriculum and the addition of a fifth year to the traditional four-year course of study.

This lithograph, created in 1856, reflects a few of the physical changes that Lee oversaw during his tenure as superintendent of West Point. Among them are a new cadet barracks (*top left*) and a riding hall (*middle right*). *(Library of Congress)*

He also compensated in part for his frequent absences from his own family by adopting an entire corps of cadets. Despite Lee's initial misgivings, he succeeded brilliantly as overseer of one of the finest military schools in the world. In June 1854, the Board of Visitors reported his "eminent qualifications," declaring that his valorous deeds in Mexico "have lost none of their lustre in the exalted position he so worthily fills."

Several milestones in Lee's life occurred during his tenure at West Point. Mary Custis, Mary Lee's mother, died on April 23, 1853. Mary Lee was shaken, her husband almost equally distraught. Of his late mother-in-law, Lee said, "She was to me all that a mother could be." She had come into Lee's life soon after the death of his own mother and had filled a great void. He would miss her. The following July he took confirmation as an Episcopalian. A year later, Custis, Lee's beloved "Boo," graduated first in his class at West Point. Meanwhile, William Henry, or "Rooney," had opted to attend Harvard, and Lee's oldest daughter Mary had gone off to school at Pelham Priory in Westchester County, New York. Lee's family was growing up and leaving home.

On April 12, 1855, it became Lee's turn to leave home—again. Lee, now with the permanent (regular army) rank of lieutenant colonel (but with the continuing brevet rank of colonel), received orders to report to the 2nd Cavalry in Louisville, Kentucky, as second in command. The newly formed regiment, commanded by Colonel Albert S. Johnston, was scheduled for subsequent duty on the Texas frontier. Mary, who was unwell, was to remain at Arlington with the younger children (Annie, Agnes, Rob, and Mildred). Lee had mixed feelings about his new posting. "The change from my present confined and sedentary life, to one more free and active, will certainly be more agreeable to my feelings and serviceable to my health," he wrote Markie Williams, his wife's cousin and his own cousin far removed. "But my happiness can never be advanced by my separation from my wife, children and friends."

At about this time in his life, Lee experienced symptoms of depression. He hated long separations from his family and being an absent parent. For a time, he again considered leaving the army and applying his engineering skills in civilian life. But the army was what he knew best, and he loved it. Lee attempted to explain his attachment to the army in a letter to Mary: "You have often heard me say that the cordiality & friendship in the Army, was the greatest attraction in the Service. It is that I believe has kept me in it so long, & it is that which makes me now fear to leave it. I do not know where I should meet with so much friendship out of it."

Lee reported to the 2nd Cavalry in Louisville on April 20, 1855, and moved west with the regiment the following summer to Fort Jefferson, outside St. Louis, Missouri. Lee's transfer from the engineers to line duty in the cavalry, at his own request, marked another important milestone in his army career. Jefferson Davis, who was then serving as secretary of war, commented that

Jefferson Davis. *(Library of Congress)*

"the son of Light-Horse Harry Lee now seemed to be in his proper element."

Before the 2nd Cavalry was deployed to the Texas frontier, Lee received orders to serve on courts-martial at Forts Leavenworth and Riley in Kansas. If Lee had hoped to see action protecting settlers from Indian attacks on the frontier, he met with instant disappointment. Much of his active-duty time during the next four years was interrupted by service on courts-martial boards—the curse of the line officer. Lee actually saw only limited service policing the frontier. His one foray—against a Comanche chief and his marauders—came out of Camp Cooper, near present-day Abilene, Texas, in the summer of 1856. In pursuit of the raiders, Lee led an expedition across 1,600 miles of West Texas wilderness, which he described as "the most barren and least inviting country I have ever seen." The Comanches got away.

Lee's time on the Texas frontier and around the court-martial circuit rank as the most unrewarding years of his career. In the East, other officers with less ability were climbing the ladder of command through political influence; in the West, he marked time, performing perfunctory duties and longing for home and family. Family problems added to his concerns. Mary's health continued to decline in general, while her rheumatism now restricted the use of her right hand and arm. Another problem was resolved in the summer of 1857. Rooney, who had been experiencing difficulties at Harvard, secured—with the help of Winfield Scott—a commission in the infantry and left the Cambridge school. Still another problem cropped up a couple of months later.

On October 21, 1857, Lee received news from Arlington that interrupted his frontier duties for the next two years: his father-in-law, George Washington Parke Custis, was dead. Lee obtained a leave of absence of one year to settle the estate. Custis had been heavily in debt and his estate was complicated. Lee's leave was extended another year. Then, on October 17, 1859, Lieutenant

A writer, painter, and historian, George Washington Parke Custis was also the builder and original owner of Arlington House. *(Library of Congress)*

James Ewell Brown (Jeb) Stuart, who had been a favorite cadet of Lee's during his superintendency at West Point, arrived at Arlington with an order for Lee to report to the secretary of war in Washington immediately. Lee did not stop to put on his uniform. He left at once.

In Washington, Lee and Stuart went first to the war office and from there to see President James Buchanan. Lee learned that abolitionist John Brown was attempting to foment an uprising of slaves at Harpers Ferry (now in West Virginia), at the confluence of the Potomac and Shenandoah Rivers. The president placed a company of U.S. Marines from Washington and four companies of Maryland and Virginia militia troops in Lee's charge, and sent him to arrest John Brown and quell the uprising. Stuart volunteered to go along.

Connecticut-born abolitionist John Brown had migrated to Kansas Territory in the mid-1850s at a time of high tension between pro- and antislavery advocates. After a mob of slavery sympathizers sacked the town of Lawrence on May 21, 1856, Brown decided he had a divine mission to exact vengeance. Three nights later, he led a retaliatory raid on a proslavery settlement at Pottawatomie Creek. The raiders dragged five men from their cabins and hacked them to death. Brown continued to terrorize proslavery factions for the next four years.

In the summer of 1859, John Brown moved to Maryland and established headquarters in a rented farmhouse across the Potomac from Harpers Ferry, the site of a Federal armory. On the night of October 16, he led his small band of sixteen whites and five blacks across the river and seized the armory. He also took sixty citizens hostage. Brown hoped that his act would incite escaped slaves to rise up and join him in forming an "army of emancipation." Brown and his band

John Brown. *(National Portrait Gallery, Washington, D.C.)*

held out in the armory against local militia elements for the rest of the night and the following day. Lee and his forces arrived on the second night.

"On arriving here on the night of the 17th," Lee reported later, "I learned that a party of insurgents, about 11 PM on the 16th, had seized the watchmen at the armory, arsenal, rifle factory and bridge across the Potomac. . . . They had despatched six men . . . to arrest the principal citizens of the neighborhood and incite the negroes to join in the insurrection." Lee surveyed the delicate situation and overnight made plans to take back the Federal armory and free the hostages.

In the morning, Lee, out of courtesy, offered the commander of the Maryland militia the honor of leading the assault. The Marylander deferred to Lee's professionals on the ground that his men had wives and children at home. Lee turned to the commander of his marine company and said, "Lieutenant [Isaac] Green, would you wish the honor of taking those men out?" With a doff of his cap, the marine accepted with gratitude.

Lee then sent Jeb Stuart to the armory with a message demanding Brown's unconditional surrender. Meanwhile, Lee positioned the marines for an immediate bayonet attack if Brown rejected his demand, as Lee figured he would. Brown tried to bargain with Stuart, which some of the hostages favored, but one voice rang out above the others. "Never mind us, fire!" Lee recognized the voice as that of Lewis Washington. "The old revolutionary blood does tell," Lee said softly. At the door to the armory, Stuart stepped aside and waved his hat.

The marines attacked with battering rams and empty rifles. Lee did not want to risk the lives of hostages to errant bullets. Cold steel would have to suffice. And it did. The marines stormed the armory and overpowered Brown and his followers in the next three minutes, killing ten of the insurgents (including two of Brown's sons), capturing Brown and the others, and freeing the hostages without injury. One marine was shot and killed, and another wounded. Brown was tried for murder, slave insurrection, and treason against the state, and was convicted and hanged on December 2, 1859.

Brown's execution made him a hero in the eyes of antislavery proponents and hastened the advent of a war to settle the slavery issue. The very fact that a white man

At Lee's orders, marines stormed the armory at Harpers Ferry where John Brown was holding his hostages.

had led the insurgency brought home to Lee the gathering crisis between the North and the South. For the present, however, Lee believed the incident at Harpers Ferry to be "the attempt of a fanatic or madman," but he viewed Brown's later adulation as a martyr in the North as a sign of a far greater evil soon to come.

On February 9, 1860, the army ordered Lee to San Antonio to take command of the military Department of Texas. Once again, he left for duty in the West, leaving family and the good life at Arlington behind. While Lee administrated the deployment of insufficient troops against a surplus of Kiowas, Comanches, and Mexicans in west Texas, the politics of an industrialized, free-farming North and an agrarian South, whose cotton fields relied on slave labor, moved the two factions closer to war in the East. Ongoing disagreements over trade tariffs and states' rights also contributed to the widening rift between North and South, but the issue of slavery was the tremor that was about to split the nation at the Mason-Dixon Line.

Lee's own views on slavery appear to have been somewhat mixed. In 1856, in a letter to Mary, he explained that, "In this enlightened age there are few, I believe, but what will acknowledge that slavery, as an institution, is a moral & political evil. . . . I think it, however, a greater evil to the white than to the black race, & while my sympathies are strongly enlisted in behalf of the latter, my sympathies are more strong for the former."

Later in that same letter, Lee turned to his religion for support: "The blacks are immeasurably better off here than in Africa, morally, socially, & physically. The painful discipline they are undergoing is necessary for their instruction as a race, & I hope will prepare and lead them to better things. How long their subjugation may be necessary is known & ordered by a wise Merciful Providence. Their emancipation will sooner result from the mild & melting influence of Christianity, than the storms & tempests of fiery Controversy."

It is generally believed—but not known for certain—that Lee freed his own slaves before departing for the Mexican War. The slaves belonging to the Custis estate, which came under Lee's purview, were freed in 1861. As the schism widened between North and South, and war seemed inevitable, Lee commented, "If the slaves of the South were mine, I would surrender them all without a struggle, to avert this war."

In light of the available evidence on Lee's attitude toward the slavery question, it seems fair to conclude that Lee, like many of his contemporaries—including Abraham Lincoln—deplored slavery but could see no immediate solution for the problem it presented. As with most things beyond his control, Lee chose to leave the solution to God.

The framers of the United States Constitution made no provisions for the secession—that is, the withdrawal—of states from the federal Union. The nationalists at the Constitutional Convention in Philadelphia in 1787 envisioned a powerful national government based on the sovereignty of the whole people, a nation indivisible. Another faction, known as the Anti-Federalists, viewed the Constitution as a compact—an agreement between two or more parties. In that case, any state could withdraw from the compact. In their eyes, the federal government was little more than an agent of the states.

The right to secession was marginally implied in the Virginia and Kentucky Resolutions of 1798, which stated that the general government held no powers beyond those specifically delegated to it. And it was certainly implied in the doctrine of nullification formulated by John C. Calhoun in 1828 for the South Carolina legislature to resist federal tariffs. The doctrine declared the tariffs null and void, and forbade their collection by state or federal officers in the state under threat of secession by South Carolina. President Andrew Jackson reacted vigorously to refute the doctrine and effectively preserved the Union—for the time being.

When the Missouri Compromise of 1820 failed to appease the concerns of both free and slave states, threats of secession grew more frequent and strident, particularly after the Mexican War. After the election of antislavery Republican candidate Abraham Lincoln in November 1860, South Carolina seceded from the Union on December 20, 1860. Over the next seven months, ten more states seceded: Mississippi, Florida, Alabama, Georgia, Louisiana, Texas, Virginia, Arkansas, North Carolina, and Tennessee.

Twenty-five states remained loyal to the Union or joined it during the hostilities that commenced on April 12, 1861: California, Connecticut, Delaware, Illinois, Indiana, Iowa, Kansas, Kentucky, Maine, Maryland, Massachusetts, Michigan, Minnesota, Missouri, Nevada (1864 statehood), New Hampshire, New Jersey, New York, Ohio, Oregon, Pennsylvania, Rhode Island, Vermont, West Virginia (1863 statehood), and Wisconsin. Of these states, Delaware, Maryland, Kentucky, and Missouri were slaveholding states bordering the newly formed Confederate States of America.

In the end, the war between the North and the South would preserve the Union and put an end to secession as an issue in constitutional deliberation.

On November 6, 1860, Republican antislavery can-

THE "SECESSION MOVEMENT".

This contemporary political cartoon portrayed secession as a doomed enterprise. The artist shows Florida, Alabama, Mississippi, and Louisiana, all represented by men riding donkeys, which symbolize the Democratic Party, following the lead of South Carolina toward a cliff. *(Library of Congress)*

didate Abraham Lincoln was elected president of the United States with only thirty-nine percent of the popular vote. Seven weeks later, South Carolina seceded from the Union, to become the first of eleven Southern states to secede. On January 9, 1861, Mississippi seceded, followed by Florida on the 10th, Alabama on the 11th, and Georgia on the 18th. On January 23, 1861, Lee wrote his son Rooney from Fort Mason, Texas:

> I can anticipate no greater calamity for the country than a dissolution of the Union. It would be an accumulation of all the evils we complain of, and I am willing to sacrifice everything but honor for its preservation. . . . Still, a Union that can only be maintained by swords and bayonets, and in which

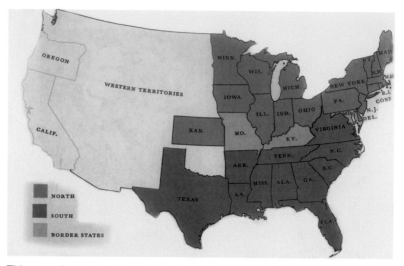

This map shows the breakdown of states that supported slavery (the South) and free states (the North) in 1861.

strife and civil war are to take the place of brotherly love and kindness, has no charm for me. . . . If the Union is dissolved, and the Government disrupted, I shall return to my native State and share the miseries of my people, and save in defense will draw my sword on none.

After thirty-two years in the service of his country, Lee, at age fifty-four, was torn between two loyalties. The nation was in tumult and events were rushing it toward war.

Louisiana seceded from the Union on January 26, and Texas proclaimed itself an independent republic for the second time on February 1, 1861. Three days later, delegates from six of the secessionist states met in Montgomery, Alabama, to form the Confederate States of America (CSA). They elected Jefferson Davis, former Mexican War hero and later U.S. secretary of war and senator from Mississippi, as their president. At the same time, Virginia sent a commission to Washington to explore the possibility of peacefully separating from the Union. Meanwhile, the army sent orders to Lee to report to Washington.

Lee arrived at Arlington on March 1 and within a week had met for three hours, behind closed doors, with General Winfield Scott. Scott likely informed Lee of his promotion to colonel (regular army) and of his appointment as commander of the 1st Cavalry. But Scott did not

The inauguration of Jefferson Davis as president of the Confederacy in Montgomery, Alabama, on February 18, 1861. *(Library of Congress)*

have to summon his fellow Virginian all the way from Texas to tell him that, so the two old friends probably spent most of the time discussing the secession and the likelihood of war. Mary Lee later reported, "My husband was summoned to Washington, where every motive and argument was used to induce him to accept command of the army destined to invade the South."

Meanwhile, Abraham Lincoln was sworn in as president on March 4, 1861. In his inaugural speech, Lincoln defended the Union, calling it perpetual and declaring secession illegal. But he further stated that "there needs to be no bloodshed or violence; and there shall be none, unless it be forced upon the national authority." On March 16, Lee accepted his promotion to colonel and command of the U.S. 1st Cavalry. He apparently ignored an offer to become a brigadier general in the Confederate Army. His commission came through, signed by President Lincoln, on March 28.

On April 12, 1861, Confederate forces commanded by Brigadier General P. G. T. Beauregard fired on Union-held Fort Sumter, South Carolina. Three days later, Lincoln called for seventy-five thousand volunteers to quell the rebellion. The divided nation was at war.

On April 17, the Virginia legislature passed an ordinance of secession. (Lee did not receive the news until two days later.) Also on the 17th, Lee received an invitation to visit Francis Preston Blair Sr., a close friend of the president, and another request to meet with Winfield Scott. The next day, Lee visited Blair at 1651 Pennsyl-

The inauguration of President Abraham Lincoln at the U.S. Capitol building in Washington, D.C., on March 4, 1861. *(Library of Congress)*

vania Avenue, in Washington, home of Blair's son, Montgomery Blair. The elder Blair, acting as the president's agent, offered Lee a promotion to major general and command of the hundred thousand-man Union army then being raised to enforce the Federal law. Lee now faced the hardest decision of his life.

At that moment, everything Lee had worked toward for his entire adult life—a supreme command with the full support of his government and the cooperation of many of his ablest comrades—was within his grasp. All he had to do was accept Blair's offer. Instead, Lee declined the offer, "stating as candidly and as courteously as I could," as he put it later, "that though opposed to secession and deprecating war, I could take no part in an invasion of the Southern States."

Lee left the Blair residence and went directly to Winfield Scott's office. When Lee told his aging mentor of his decision, Scott, visibly moved, said, "Lee, you have made the greatest mistake of your life; but I feared it would be so." The morals and ethics of Lee's decision are eternally arguable. Despite the oath he had sworn to defend the United States of America, Lee believed that his first loyalty lay with his home state of Virginia. Forced to choose between his nation and his state, home, and family, he followed his conscience.

6

A Shot for the Southern Cause

Winfield Scott was a Virginian who had chosen to remain loyal to the Union, but his name, unlike Lee's, did not extend its roots in Virginia back more than two centuries to the 1640s. Neither was his family name historically linked to George Washington and other honor-bound Virginians such as Patrick Henry, James Madison, and Thomas Jefferson. Nor did his home stand on a hill overlooking the Potomac, across the river from Washington, at the forefront of possible extinction. Scott believed in the Union and stood by it. Lee's decision to stand by Virginia pained him, yet he understood it.

"There are times," Scott reportedly advised his protégé, "when every officer in the United States service should fully determine what course he will pursue and frankly declare it. No one should continue in gov-

Lee tendered his letter of resignation from the United States Army, in which he had served for more than thirty-two years, shortly after learning that his home state of Virginia had seceded from the Union. *(National Archives)*

ernment employ without being actively employed." In other words, if Lee chose not to lead a Union army against the South, he should resign promptly. The two officers parted amiably, and Lee left Washington for the last time. With a heavy heart, he rode back to Arlington to ponder his future.

Lee learned of Virginia's secession the next morning, April 19, 1861. That night, after midnight, he wrote a letter to U.S. secretary of war Simon Cameron in which he simply stated, "I have the honor to tender the resignation of my commission as Colonel of the 1st Regt. of Cavalry." And to General Scott, his superior, mentor, and advancer of his career, he wrote a second letter in which he stated, in part, that for

> more than 30 years, I have experienced nothing but kindness from my superiors, and a most cordial friendship from my companions. To no one [General] have I been as much indebted as to yourself for uniform kindness and consideration, and it has always been my ardent desire to meet your approbation. I shall carry with me to the grave the most grateful recollections of your kind consideration, and your name and fame will always be dear to me. Save in defence of my native State, I desire never again to draw my sword.

When Lee finished writing the two letters, he went downstairs at Arlington House and said to his wife, "Well, Mary, the question is settled. Here is my letter of resignation and a letter I have written General Scott."

Later that day, Lee received an invitation to meet with Virginia governor John Letcher in Richmond, Virginia. On April 23, 1861, Letcher asked Lee to accept command of "the military and naval forces of Virginia." Lee accepted. Within three days, Lee had resigned from the United States Army (USA), in which he had served faithfully for thirty-two years, and had joined a second army that was dedicated to the defeat of the first.

Two days later, Lee still hoped for some turn of events that might turn back the forces of war that were engulfing the nation, but he recognized the futility of such hopes. On April 25, he wrote: "No earthly act would give me so much pleasure as to restore peace to my country, but I fear it is now out of the power of man, and in God alone must be our trust. I think our policy should be purely on the defensive, to resist aggression and allow time to allay the passions and permit reason to resume her sway." He set to work at once, organizing Virginia's military strength and surveying the fields upon which he anticipated that future battles for the Confederacy would be fought. Even as he hoped for the impossible, he was preparing for the inevitable.

On May 2, Custis Lee, now twenty-nine years old, resigned as first lieutenant in the engineer corps and accepted a cap-tain's commission in the Confederate engineers. Rooney joined the CSA cav-alry as a captain. Lee's brother Smith entered the Con-federate navy and sent three of his sons into the CSA, including the soon-to-become re-nowned Fitzhugh Lee. Lee's seven-teen-year-old son

Rob Lee, the youngest of the Lee boys, was the general's only son not to immediately join the war effort.

Rob remained at the University of Virginia on the advice of his father. Mildred, the baby of the family, stayed in school at Winchester. The other girls remained with their mother at Arlington, making preparations to leave the family estate. For the Lees, war was a family affair.

While Lee administrated Virginia's mobilization in Richmond, Mary Lee remained at her beloved Arlington House. By mid-May 1861, however, Arlington became unsafe for Confederate families or sympathizers. Mary withdrew to Ravensworth with her daughter Mildred and then to Kinloch (home of one of Lee's distant cousins in Fauquier County) with her daughter Mary. By October 1861, Mary had moved again to Shirley, the Carter family home on the James River, a few miles below Richmond.

The pressures of Federal movements forced Mary to continue to move. From Shirley she took her family to White House, a Custis property in New Kent County then controlled by her second son, Rooney. With the imminent approach of Federal troops in June 1862, she posted a note on the front door at White House and left again, a step ahead of the enemy soldiers. The note read, "Northern soldiers who profess to reverence Washington, forebear to desecrate the home of his first married life, the property of his wife, now owned by her descendants." From White House, Mary moved to Marlbourne, a plantation in Hanover County, Virginia.

In the autumn of 1862, Mary and her daughter Agnes moved to Hickory Hill, the plantation of Charlotte

After Mary Lee abandoned White House, the estate eventually became Union headquarters for General McClellan, which most likely explains the American flag and the soldiers pictured here on the porch. Despite Mary's note and explicit Union orders, the house was eventually razed. *(Library of Congress)*

Wickham Lee's family in Hanover County. Charlotte, or "Chass," was Rooney's wife and thus Mary's daughter-in-law. Shortly thereafter, Lee advised Mary not to move into Richmond, as living there would be too dangerous. Mary, with a mind of her own, moved into Richmond and remained there for the next year and a half.

In July 1864, Lee finally persuaded Mary to leave Richmond, and she moved with her daughters Mildred and Agnes to Bremo, the estate of a friend in Fluvanna County. The Lees returned to Richmond after the war. During her wartime odyssey, Mary was hobbled by arthritis and confined to a wheelchair for the last two years.

On May 14, 1861, the Confederate War Department appointed Lee brigadier general in the CSA. Two days later, the Confederate Congress authorized his advancement to the rank of full general, effective on August 31,

1861. (He would then become the third-ranking Confederate officer behind Samuel Cooper and Albert Sidney Johnston.) Walter H. Taylor, a future member of Lee's staff, recalled his first meeting with Lee in early May. "Admirably proportioned, of graceful and dignified carriage," Taylor wrote, "with strikingly handsome features, bright and penetrating eyes, his iron-gray hair closely cut, his face cleanly shaved except for a mustache, he appeared every inch a soldier and born to command."

On May 20, 1861, the Confederate Congress voted to move its government to Richmond, Virginia. The new capital was now within 106 miles of Washington, D.C. Ever afterward, Richmond became an overriding objective of Union strategy. To complete the reconstitution of the Confederacy, Virginia military forces transferred to the CSA on May 25.

General Lee occupied this brick townhouse at 707 East Franklin Street while living in Richmond.

Lee spent his first seven weeks as a Confederate general tied to a desk and mired in organizational paperwork. The new capital of the Confederacy was the third-largest city in the South—behind New Orleans and

Richmond's Tredegar Iron Works. *(Library of Congress)*

Charleston—with a population of some 38,000. A busy port city on the James River, it was well on the way to becoming a city of industry, as evidenced by the spewing smoke stacks of the Tredegar Iron Works. On July 21, when Confederate forces under generals P. G. T. Beauregard and Joseph E. Johnston defeated a Union army under Major General Irvin McDowell at Manassas Junction, Virginia, in the first major engagement of the war, Lee could only listen to reports of the action from a distance. Among the Confederate highlights of the battle was Brigadier General Thomas J. Jackson's strong defense of Henry House Hill, for which he won the enduring sobriquet of "Stonewall" Jackson.

From his small office on the fourth floor of the Mechanics Institute in Richmond, Lee wrote Mary of the "glorious victory" and cautioned her not to "grieve for the brave dead." Instead, he revealed evidence of his own way of dealing with the inevitable fatalities of war. "Sorrow for those who are left behind—friends, relatives, family," he wrote. "The former are at rest. The latter must suffer." Lee's organizational and recruiting efforts had played an important part in the South's first major victory, but Lee did not entertain the least notion of fighting the war from behind four walls and a desk. "I wished to partake in the struggle," he added, "and am mortified at my absence."

A week later, on July 28, CSA president Jefferson Davis, who was well aware of the treasure he had in Robert E. Lee, finally found a field assignment for him. Davis sent Lee to western Virginia, where Union forces under Major General George B. McClellan had invaded the state and were threatening key railroad lines. Confederate defenses under three quarrelsome, uncooperative generals were falling apart. Lee's job was to establish order out of chaos and turn back the Federals. He devised an intricate plan to recover lost territory and launched a two-pronged attack at Cheat Mountain and Elkwater, only to be repulsed by Union troops under Brigadier General Joseph J. Reynolds. Badly trained, poorly equipped troops and flawed leadership, coupled with heavy rains and a sea of mud, resulted in a poorly executed assault, forcing Lee to withdraw to Huntersville in humbling embarrassment after the battle of Cheat Mountain (September 10–14, 1861).

Edward A. Pollard, the influential editor of the Richmond *Examiner*, expressed an opinion of Lee shared by many Southerners after his failure at Cheat Mountain. He characterized the Lee of September–October 1861 as "a general who had never fought a battle . . . and whose extreme tenderness of blood induced him to depend exclusively on the resources of strategy, to essay the achievement of victories without the cost of life." The Richmond newspapers began calling him "Granny" Lee.

Lee, humiliated, could only hope to turn the negative lessons of Cheat Mountain into positives in some future battle—if, he perhaps thought, he ever got another field command. He returned to Richmond with his tail between his legs and a new gray beard on his chin, color-coordinated with the shade of his uniform jacket and reflective of the burden of command. He would wear it for the rest of his life.

After his inauspicious beginning as a Confederate commander, Lee did not stay in Richmond for long. On November 5, 1861, President Davis relegated him to mundane duties overseeing coastal defense work in South Carolina, Georgia, and Florida, where he quickly came under further criticism for abandoning St. Simon and Jekyll Islands, off the Georgia coast, and the mainland port of Brunswick. Reacting to a Federal threat against Port Royal, South Carolina, Lee repositioned coastal defenses upriver, laying bare the barrier islands and coastal plains and infuriating many influential Confederates. For five months, he worked in the face of local criticism and apathy. Characteristically, Lee did his best under trying circumstances and established the beginnings of a practical chain of defenses.

To Georgia governor Joseph Brown, Lee complained,

"I find it impossible to obtain guns to secure it as I desire, and now everything is required to fortify this city [Savannah]." But Lee's defensive improvements helped to put off the fall of Savannah until 1864.

In the course of his duties, Lee visited his father's grave on Georgia's Cumberland Island, which he found "marked by a plain marble slab" and surrounded by a beautiful garden "inclosed by the finest [wild olive] hedge I have ever seen." During this same time, Lee came across a four-year-old gray stallion named Greenbriar, who had once been called Jeff Davis. He bought the horse for $200, renamed him Traveller, and rode him the rest of his days.

On March 2, 1862, President Davis recalled Lee to Richmond. For the South, the military situation had taken a turn for the worse. In the West, a Union army under Brigadier General Ulysses S. Grant—the man whom Lee had known in Mexico as Lieutenant Sam Grant—had captured Forts Henry and Donelson in western Tennessee. Their capture opened up a large stretch of the Mississippi Valley to the Federals. In the East, Major General George McClellan, now in command of the Union Army of the Potomac, was assembling a force of one hundred five thousand men on Virginia's York Peninsula, between the James and York Rivers, for an eventual advance on Richmond. To defend the capital against the developing Federal threat, the Confederates could field an army of no more than sixty thousand troops. Jefferson Davis desperately needed some sound

Lee astride his famous horse Traveller, whom the general described in a postwar letter to Markie Williams: "If I were an artist like you I would draw a true picture of Traveller—representing his fine proportions, muscular figure, deep chest and short back, strong haunches . . . quick eye, small feet, and black mane and tail. . . . But I am no artist; I can only say that he is a Confederate gray."

military advice. He appointed Lee his military advisor.

Lee soon discovered that no love was lost between Davis and Johnston. In his role as military advisor, one of Lee's most important duties was to act as a buffer

Lee's close friend and trusted general, Joseph E. Johnston. *(National Portrait Gallery, Washington, D.C.)*

between the two Confederate leaders, who simply did not like each other. Lee greased the wheels of high command and kept them turning at a critical time in the war. He also contributed to the South's ability to wage war by drafting the first conscription (draft) law in American history. The enlistments of many volunteers were expiring and few volunteers were coming forward to replace them. Lee drafted an act that called for all white males between the ages of eighteen and thirty-five to serve for three years in the military, and for the service of all one-year volunteers to be extended for two years.

Lee's role as advisor enabled him to see the war from the highest command level as it unfolded before his eyes, an experience that would prove invaluable to the future field commander. His long-awaited opportunity to command an army in the field arrived suddenly on May 31, 1862. At the battle of Seven Pines (or Fair Oaks) that day, Joe Johnston suffered severe wounds while trying to halt McClellan's drive on Richmond. Davis immediately named Lee to head Johnston's army, which Lee renamed the Army of Northern Virginia—a name that was intended to spur its men to retake that region.

Later, in a Richmond hospital, Johnston told a visitor, "The shot that struck me down is the best that has been fired for the Southern cause yet, for I possess in no degree the confidence of our government, and now they have in place one who does."

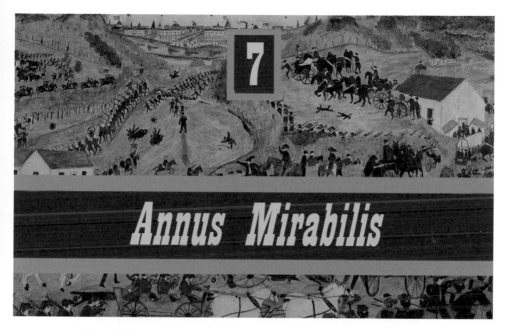

Annus Mirabilis

Confederate president Jefferson Davis's confidence in Robert E. Lee was justly placed, as Lee brilliantly demonstrated in the coming year. *Annus mirabilis* means "year of wonders or miracles" in Latin and is sometimes ascribed to Robert E. Lee's first year of command in the Civil War. Lee took command of the Army of Northern Virginia on June 1, 1862, and in the following twelve months, his leadership worked one wonder after another. His miracle working started with a string of running clashes known as the Seven Days campaign (June 25–July 1, 1862).

During Lee's first year as a Confederate officer, he had not won the approval—let alone the admiration—of most Southerners. His performance in western Virginia had been highly suspect, and his later work on

Stonewall Jackson, legendary among his troops for his bravery, was successful in the Shenandoah Valley largely due to his willingness to use maps and learn the terrain.

coastal defenses on the southeastern seaboard had met with strong criticism. On the other hand, while Lee served as military advisor to Davis, Stonewall Jackson's successful campaign in the Shenandoah Valley in the spring of 1862 owed much of its success to Lee's ability to recognize opportunities in secondary theaters of operation. Lee had devised Jackson's Shenandoah campaign to divert three Federal armies from joining McClellan's Peninsula campaign in a drive against Richmond. Much like his future adversary Sam Grant, Lee possessed a rare ability to see a battlefield in its entirety and to position firepower where it was most needed.

Lee strongly believed an offensive strategy aimed at the total destruction of the enemy's armies was essential to winning the war. He knew the South could not match the manpower and equipment of the North in a pro-tracted defensive war. Lee also knew his views were contrary to those of President Davis, who felt the South could win a defensive war of wills over the North. Nonetheless, with elements of McClellan's army within seven miles of Richmond, Lee's first thoughts as a new field general were to "change the character of the war." To defend Richmond, he planned to go on the offense. He briefed Davis on his plan to break the Union grip on the Confederate capital: "It will require 100,000 men to resist the regular siege of Richmond, which perhaps would only prolong not save it. I am preparing a line that I can hold with part of our forces in front, while with the rest I will endeavor to make diversion to bring McClellan out."

While preparing a defensive line—entrenching—during his first three weeks in command, Lee drew more criticism from his detractors. The Richmond *Examiner* greeted his appointment to command ingloriously, sug-gesting that the army would thereafter not be allowed to fight, only to dig, "spades & shovels being the only implements Gen. Lee knew anything about."

On June 10, Lee ordered Major General Jeb Stuart and 1,200 cavalrymen on a reconnaissance ride toward the enemy's right to observe McClellan's positioning.

Stuart and his troopers rode around the entire Union army, covering more than one hundred miles in three days (July 12–15) in one of the most astonishing missions of the war. Stuart found the bulk of McClellan's army, about seventy-five thousand troops, positioned south of the Chickahominy River, preparing to lay siege to Richmond. Only Major General Fitz-John Porter's Union V Corps, about twenty-five thousand troops, remained north of the river on McClellan's right flank, which Stuart observed was unattended. Stuart returned to report his finding to Lee on July 15. Lee went forward with his attack plan, which he scheduled to begin on July 26 with a surprise attack on Mechanicsville. But McClellan attacked first.

On June 25, McClellan launched a probing attack at Oak Grove, due east of Richmond, which marked the beginning of the Seven Days campaign. Fearing himself outnumbered, McClellan made no attempt to break through the Confederate defenses and drive into Richmond. Lee suspected that the enemy had somehow learned of his plan of operation, but he remained undeterred. That evening, Lee wrote President Davis, "I have determined to make no change in the plan."

Leaving a small force of twenty-five thousand men to guard Richmond against McClellan's main force of seventy-five thousand—a huge gamble—Lee shifted sixty-five thousand troops northward to strike McClellan's exposed right flank of about twenty-five thousand men. Lee's striking force included three of

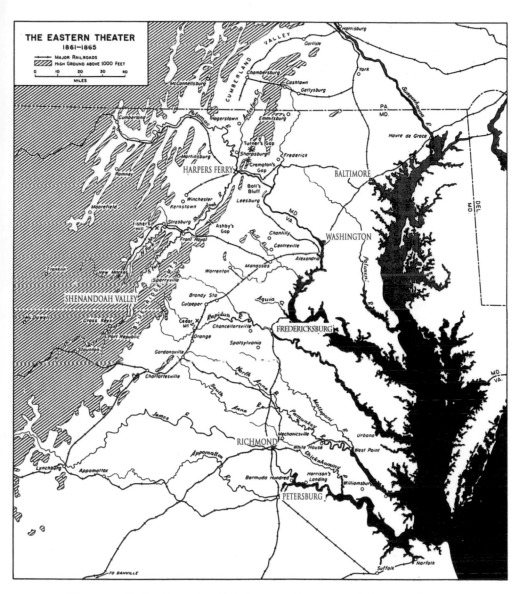

THE EASTERN THEATER
1861–1865

MAJOR RAILROADS
HIGH GROUND ABOVE 1000 FEET

0   10   20   30   40
MILES

Stonewall Jackson's divisions of some eighteen thousand men from the Shenandoah Valley. Lee planned to destroy Porter's V Corps in a coordinated surprise attack from the west and the north, and then drive against McClellan's main body from the rear, forcing his Army of the Potomac southward and off the peninsula.

At 3:00 PM on June 26, after Jackson's divisions had

failed to arrive as planned, Lieutenant General Ambrose P. Hill attacked alone with his division from the west. Hill failed to destroy Porter's corps in the battle of Mechanicsville (June 26), but forced Porter to withdraw to Gaines's Mill. The next day, Lee continued his attack on Porter with the divisions of Generals Daniel H. Hill, Jackson, Ambrose P. Hill (no relation to Daniel H.), and James Longstreet in the battle of Gaines's Mill (June 27). Lee's forces smashed through the Union defenses in perhaps the largest frontal assault of the whole war, forcing McClellan to withdraw toward the James River.

After a day's lull in the fighting, Lee realized he had McClellan on the run and gave chase. On June 29 and 30, he joined his enemy in battles at Peach Orchard, Savage's Station, White Oak Swamp, Frayser's Farm (or Glendale), and in a host of lesser skirmishes, but failed to cut off his fleeing foe. The next day, a frustrated Lee ordered another frontal assault against a strongly held Union position at Malvern Hill. The attackers suffered heavy casualties. "It was not war," Lieutenant General Daniel H. Hill said afterward. "It was murder." The Confederate onslaught that ended seven days of savage fighting again failed to halt McClellan's retreat. Lee failed in his final effort to destroy the Army of the Potomac, which withdrew to Harrison's Landing on the James River, where it remained under the protection of Union gunboats until mid-August.

Although he had not been able to destroy McClellan's army, Lee's big gamble had paid off handsomely. His

McClellan's Federal troops retreat from the battle at Savage's Station during the Seven Days campaign. *(Library of Congress)*

aggressiveness and boldness had saved Richmond in seven days and had effectively ended McClellan's campaign on the peninsula. But the victory came at a high price. A week of offensive action had cost him some twenty thousand casualties, against Union losses of about sixteen thousand. Despite losing almost a quarter of his army in casualties, Lee, in victory, won the hearts of Confederates everywhere. Yet, in a letter to Mary, he confided, "Our success has not been as great or complete as I could have desired." And in his official report, Lee wrote, "Under ordinary circumstances the Federal Army should have been destroyed."

In his battles to save Richmond, Lee felt that Jackson had not performed as well as he had expected—probably because of extreme fatigue—and that several other of his subordinate commanders had let him down. The first battles under his command served as a learning period for Lee, and he was willing to make any adjustments needed. For now, Southerners were hailing him as a hero. Even the Richmond *Dispatch* praised him in print: "No captain that ever lived could have planned or executed a better plan." Lee's plan had thwarted the enemy threat to Richmond for the moment, but few could doubt that the Confederate capital would remain the Union's most sought-after prize.

In Washington, President Lincoln recognized the need for better professional generalship. On June 26, he had already called Major General John Pope from the West to command the newly formed Union Army of Virginia, comprising the commands of Major Generals Irvin McDowell, John C. Fremont, and Nathaniel P. Banks. After Lee's strategic victory in the Seven Days campaign, Lincoln reestablished the position of general in chief of the Union armies and appointed Major General Henry W. Halleck, a military theoretician known as "Old Brains," to fill it. (McClellan had vacated the position when he embarked on his Peninsula campaign.) On

August 3, Halleck ordered McClellan's Army of the Potomac back to Washington.

In the vicinity of Richmond, Lee made some changes of his own, dismissing several inept generals and restructuring his army into two corps-size wings under Jackson and James Longstreet. Lee did not criticize Jackson's performance or late arrivals in two of the Seven Days battles, but he reduced Jackson's command from fourteen brigades to seven and upped Longstreet's command from six brigades to twenty-eight. Jackson probably got Lee's message. While making his changes, Lee kept a close eye on Federal troop movements through accounts published in Northern newspapers that filtered into the South and through intelligence reports.

On July 13, Lee sent Jackson with twelve thousand troops to observe Pope's activities in northern Virginia. Lee followed slowly with the rest of his army, leaving twenty thousand troops to defend Richmond. When McClellan remained in place at Harrison's Landing, Lee sent A. P. Hill to join Jackson with twelve thousand more reinforcements. Lee's instructions to Jackson stated: "I must now leave the matter to your reflection and good judgment. Make up your mind what is best to be done in all circumstances . . . and let me hear the result at which you arrive." Lee planned the operations of his army and positioned his units for optimum effectiveness, but allowed his battlefield commanders wide latitude in executing his aims. On August 9, Jackson engaged a detachment of Pope's army at Cedar Mountain in a sharp battle. Jackson, realizing he had met only the vanguard of Pope's army, then retreated across the Rapidan River.

Meanwhile, Lee learned that the Army of the Potomac was withdrawing from the York Peninsula to join Pope. Together, the two Union armies would total about one hundred fifty thousand men, and they would face his own army that now numbered about fifty-five thousand. Lee quickly put together a plan to crush Pope's army before McClellan's forces could join it. His plan called for Jackson to move north, then east, to get behind Pope, after which Lee, with Longstreet, would follow to join Jackson in a two-sided attack on Pope.

On August 25 and 26, Jackson moved north, covering fifty-four miles in two days, and wiped out the Federal supply depot at Manassas. He then took up concealed defensive positions west of the old Manassas (Bull Run) battlefield. Pope, enraged at the loss of his supply depot, hastened north in pursuit of Jackson's marauders, refusing to believe Longstreet's corps could be anywhere in the area. Jackson attacked Pope near Groveton to divert his attention, while Lee and Longstreet, screened by the Bull Run Mountains, slipped through Thoroughfare Gap and struck Pope's left flank. In the ensuing Second Battle of Manassas (or Bull Run) (August 29–30, 1862), Lee's Army of Northern Virginia rolled up Pope's Army of Virginia and threw it back across the old Manassas battlefield.

One Confederate soldier lucidly described firing at the Federals as they retreated, "so near and so thick" that "every shot took effect. . . . We shot into this mass as fast as we could load until our guns got so hot we had at times to wait for them to cool." Soon after the battle, a Union survivor of Longstreet's attack recalled the horror of his recent experience. "I saw the men dropping on all sides," he wrote, "canteens struck and flying to pieces, haversacks cut off, rifles knocked to pieces, it was a perfect hail of bullets. I was expecting to get it every second, but on, on, I went, the balls hissing by my head."

Amid such chaos, the second battle of Manassas ended in a Federal rout. Union losses totaled more than sixteen thousand men; the Confederates lost about 9,200. Significantly, the capital under imminent threat now became Washington instead of Richmond.

After the second battle of Manassas, Lee, pursuing his conviction that a quick victory over the North was

The bloody and chaotic second battle of Manassas. *(Library of Congress)*

the South's only hope of winning the war, crossed the Potomac into Maryland and began his first invasion of the North on September 5, 1862. In Washington, McClellan absorbed the remnants of Pope's army into his Army of the Potomac and began moving slowly northwest toward Frederick, Maryland, with about eighty-five thousand troops. (Pope was assigned to Indian fighting in Minnesota.) At the same time, Lee divided his army of sixty-five thousand, sending Jackson's corps west to attack Harpers Ferry and moving his remaining fifty-five thousand troops from Frederick to Hagerstown, Maryland. The capture of Harpers Ferry would open up a Confederate supply route to the Shenandoah Valley, a prize which Lee felt was worth the risk of splitting his forces. In Washington, President Lincoln welcomed Lee's invasion as a chance to punish the rebels and told McClellan not to let Lee "get off without being hurt."

McClellan's advance elements reached Frederick on September 12, where they found a copy of Lee's orders where a careless Confederate staff officer had dropped them. The orders outlined Confederate dispositions and movements. When presented with Lee's operational guidelines, a delighted McClellan told a subordinate, "Here is a paper with which if I cannot whip Bobbie Lee, I will be willing to go home." At that point, Lee's army was spread out over twenty-five miles and separated by an unfordable river, completely at McClellan's mercy. A less cautious general might have capitalized on such an advantage, but it took McClellan two days to advance ten miles to the passes over South Mountain.

On September 14, Lee's covering forces delayed McClellan's advance at South Mountain, while Jackson's corps captured Harpers Ferry after heavy fighting that day and the next. Lee initially planned to retreat before the numerically superior Federal forces. When he learned that Jackson was rushing to join him, however, Lee decided to give battle. The war would be won only by destroying the enemy. He took up defensive positions west of Antietam Creek, near the Maryland village of Sharpsburg. With the Potomac River and only a single avenue of escape at his back, he awaited General McClellan's sluggish advance.

The Army of the Potomac began arriving on September 15. McClellan planned on rolling up Lee's left flank with three corps, while a fourth corps attacked across the fordable creek to pin Lee's right and two corps remained in reserve. Instead of attacking on September 16, when he had Lee at about a two-to-one manpower disadvantage, the cautious Federal commander spent the day perfecting his plan for an attack the next day. McClellan struck at dawn on September 17. By then, Stonewall Jackson had arrived from Harpers Ferry to reinforce Lee, and the battle of Antietam—or Sharpsburg, as it was called in the South—was joined. This recollection of a Union soldier who fought at Antietam epitomizes the battlefield behavior of those who took part in the savage battle: "The truth is, when bullets are whack-

Civil War photographer Matthew Brady took some of the most famous and startling images of the war. This photograph of dead Confederate soldiers from Stonewall Jackson's unit graphically depicts the terrible silence that fell after Antietam's bloody battle. *(Library of Congress)*

ing against tree-trunks and solid shot are cracking skulls like egg-shells, the consuming passion in the breast of the average man is to get out of the way. Between the physical fear of going forward and the moral fear of turning back, there is a predicament of exceptional awkwardness."

But the men in blue charged forward, and the men in gray shoved them back; soldiers on both sides clashed again and again from dawn till dusk. Only the skillful field generalship of Lee and his commanders, combined with the courage of his men, averted the utter destruction of the Army of Northern Virginia. "It is beyond all wonder," a Union officer wrote after the battle, "how such men as the rebel troops can fight on as they do; that, filthy, sick, hungry, and miserable, they should prove such heroes in fight, is past explanation."

The one-day battle at Antietam Creek holds the sinister distinction of being the bloodiest single day of the war. Lee lost almost fourteen thousand men, including twenty-seven hundred dead; McClellan more than twelve thousand, with over two thousand killed. Lee remained in position during the day on September 18, then withdrew silently during the night and returned to Virginia. Both sides claimed victory in what was effectively a draw. Antietam demonstrated clearly that Lee's hope for a quick, decisive triumph over the Union was not going to happen. Furthermore, hopes for European recognition of the South as a viable new nation and support for its cause faded.

Until this point, President Lincoln, like most Americans, had seen the war as an effort to keep the Union together. Lincoln had been under pressure from abolitionists to outlaw slavery, but he had refused to do so, worried he would alienate slaveholding states that had not seceded. But during the summer of 1862, Lincoln began to consider a plan to outlaw slavery in the Confederate states. The aftermath of Antietam seemed a propitious time, and on September 22, he read to his cabinet a preliminary draft of the Emancipation Proclamation. It would go into effect on the first day of January, 1863, and its purpose was to free the slaves of all rebellious states—but not the slaves in Union states—in order to help end the war. With this announcement, it became clear that the war would continue.

This 1863 painting, fancifully imagining an exhausted Lincoln crafting the Emancipation Proclamation, is full of symbolic imagery, such as the hanged bust of President Buchanan, the skewed scales of justice, and the rail-splitter's maul on the floor. *(Library of Congress)*

After taking command in June 1862, Lee had driven the Union troops out of Virginia and had raised the hopes of Southerners for an ultimate victory. He had also pushed his army too hard and too far and had diminished its ranks greatly. After Antietam, he spent the next two months rebuilding and refurbishing his army near the town of Fredericksburg, Virginia. In December 1862, the revitalized Army of Northern Virginia consisted of the I and II Corps, led by Longstreet and Jackson, respectively, and a cavalry division under Jeb Stuart. In mid-October, Jeb had again showed his worth in a raid to sever the Union supply line at a bridge near Chambersburg, Pennsylvania. During the raid, he completed a second ride around McClellan's army.

Meanwhile, in Washington, President Lincoln, his patience exhausted with the slow-moving McClellan, named Major General Ambrose E. Burnside to replace him as commander of the Army of the Potomac on November 7. Burnside immediately moved to the Rappahannock River, at Fredericksburg, which he planned to cross and advance on Richmond. He arrived at the four-hundred-foot-wide river on November 17, but the lack of a pontoon train to cross it created a delay of almost a month. The delay allowed Lee to establish Longstreet's I Corps on the high ground at Marye's Heights on his left (northwest) flank, and to position Jackson's II Corps downstream to anchor his right. Burnside finally bridged the river on the night of December 10 and moved into attack positions opposite Fredericksburg.

On the morning of December 13, Burnside's Army of the Potomac—now one hundred twenty thousand strong—attacked. Burnside mounted repeated frontal attacks with three Grand Divisions: the Left, commanded by Major General William B. Franklin; the Center, led by Major General Joseph "Fighting Joe" Hooker; and the Right, under Major General Edwin V. Sumner. In two days of fighting, the Federals pounded Lee's defenses time after time, and time after time were repulsed. Lee, watching the panoramic scene from a promontory known henceforth as "Lee's Hill," turned to a subordinate and said, "It is well that war is so terrible—we should grow too fond of it."

Burnside withdrew across the river on the night of December 14–15, attacked again downriver with the same results, then ordered an end to the slaughter and withdrew for good. Lee did not pursue the retreating Federals, feeling that his army was too small in numbers to exploit his victory successfully. Some feel that by not doing so, Lee missed his one clear chance to end the war. As it was, the Federals had more than 12,500 casualties;

Lee and his staff observe the fighting at Fredericksburg from what would come to be known as "Lee's Hill." *(Library of Congress)*

the Confederates, over 5,300. In triumph, Lee expressed disappointment. "They suffered heavily as far as the battle went," he said, "but it did not go far enough to satisfy me. The contest will now have to be renewed, but on what field I cannot say." Lee's dismal appraisal did not take into account the effect of his victory on Northern morale.

In Washington, public disappointment and dissatisfaction weighed heavily on President Lincoln. "If there is a worse place than Hell," he told a friend, "I am in it." But he stayed the Union course and issued the final version of the Emancipation Proclamation on January 1, 1863. He also replaced Burnside with Joe Hooker on January 26.

Lee's convincing triumph at Fredericksburg ended the fighting in Virginia for the winter of 1862–1863, but surviving the harsh season was a battle in itself for Lee and his army. Potentially aggressive Federal movements forced Lee to detach Longstreet's corps to the south side of the lower James River, while the rest of his hungry army foraged about the Virginia countryside to sustain itself. Lee himself contracted a heavy cold and—worse— began to show signs of a weakening heart. On April 10, 1863, however, his doctor reported him improved and said, "He is cheerful and we all feel hopeful and determined and expect to win more victories over our insolent and wicked foes." Fighting Joe Hooker took an opposite view.

With the spring thaws, Virginia's roads became usable again for the tread of an army on the march. Joe Hooker used them to move the bulk of his rejuvenated one hundred thirty thousand-man army up the Rappahannock and around Lee's sixty thousand-man army at Fredericksburg. Hooker left a strong force across the river from Lee to pin the Confederate army in place. On April 30, Hooker assembled his flanking force at Chancellorsville, a crossroads town about ten miles to Lee's rear. He hoped to lure Lee into withdrawing or attacking at a disadvantage. But Lee did not rise to Hooker's bait.

On May 2, Lee sent Stonewall Jackson's II Corps on a wide flanking movement to his left with more than half of his available strength. He left Major General Jubal A. Early with ten thousand men on Marye's Heights, in front of Hooker's forty thousand-man pinning force led by Major General John Sedgwick. It was a daring move on Lee's part and violated the cardinal military maxim of never splitting a force while a battle was ongoing. Despite a two-to-one numerical superiority, Hooker opted to fight a defensive action. At dusk, Jackson began rolling up the right side of Hooker's flanking force. In the gloaming, one of Jackson's men mistook him for a Union soldier and shot him, mortally wounding him. Meanwhile, Sedgwick pushed Early steadily westward.

On May 3, Lee, after satisfying himself that Hooker's flanking force posed no immediate threat, shifted some of his troops from II Corps to reinforce Early, leaving Jeb Stuart and twenty-five thousand men to watch Hooker. The next day, Lee's forces defeated Sedgwick at Salem Church to end the awkward battle of Chancellorsville

Lee's strategy at Chancelloroviile, marking one of the most innovative and audacious moves of the war, led to a surprising victory for the Confederacy. However, the loss of Stonewall Jackson to friendly fire, as portrayed in this painting, was a brutal blow to Lee's campaign. *(Library of Congress)*

(May 2–4, 1863). Hooker began withdrawing the next night. The battle cost Hooker seventeen thousand casualties. Lee's losses totaled thirteen thousand in another stunning triumph.

Many military analysts herald Chancellorsville as Lee's greatest victory. It indeed confirmed his standing as the premier Confederate field commander. Lee himself again opined gloomily. "At Chancellorsville we gained another victory," he commented later, "our people were wild with delight—I, on the contrary, was more depressed than after Fredericksburg; our loss was severe, and again we had gained not an inch of ground and the enemy could not be pursued." Six days after the battle, on May 10, Lee suffered another loss when Stonewall Jackson died of his wounds. Lee had lost his strong right arm and one of the most popular commanders of the war.

As the summer of 1863 approached, the war outside Virginia was going badly for the South everywhere, most critically at Vicksburg, Mississippi, where Sam Grant and a Union army of sixty thousand bluejackets held the city under siege. The loss of the city would open up the entire Mississippi River to the Federals and effectively end the South's chances for anything be-yond a negotiated conclusion to hostilities. To Jefferson Davis, Lee proposed a second invasion of the North to draw Federal forces away from Richmond. Otherwise, Lee argued, Hooker's army "will take its own time to prepare and strengthen itself to renew its advance upon Richmond, and force this army back within the en-trenchments of that city." Lee's strategy was, as always, one of offensive defense. Davis agreed with him, and Lee prepared to move north with his army in June.

On June 3, 1863—one year and two days after the start of the year of wonders—Lee launched a second invasion of the North from Fredericksburg with an army of about seventy-five thousand. In Pennsylvania, he would find it harder to work his miracles.

Lee's Worst Battle

After Chancellorsville, Lee reorganized his forces again. This time, he divided his army of seventy-five thousand men into three corps. He kept Lieutenant General James Longstreet in command of I Corps, appointed Lieutenant General Richard S. Ewell to replace Jackson as head of II Corps, and named Lieutenant General A. P. Hill to lead III Corps. When his second invasion of the North got underway on June 3, 1863, Lee began shifting his forces from behind the Rappahannock River at Fredericksburg, aiming them northwest toward the Shenandoah Valley. He intended to march north up the valley and cross the Potomac River west of the Blue Ridge Mountains. Lee assigned Jeb Stuart and his cavalry division to screen his movements east of the mountains.

Longstreet led off, pausing at Culpeper while Ewell passed through to clear the lower valley of Federal troops. Hill remained at Fredericksburg to keep an eye on Hooker's Yankees across the Rappahannock. Lee and his staff left Fredericksburg on June 6 and arrived at Culpeper the next morning. Lee's initial movements went off smoothly, allowing no real opportunity for Hooker to attack his strung-out Confederates.

One of Lee's great strengths was his strong subordinates. Longstreet and Stuart were two of the best. James Longstreet was an imposing figure—over six feet tall, with long, dark auburn hair and a dark, steady stare. His heavy frame tended toward—but stayed shy of—portliness. Outwardly gruff but inwardly kindhearted, his troops knew him affectionately as "Old Pete." He fought in every major battle of the Mexican War, earned brevets to captain and major, and was wounded while carrying the colors in the attack on Chapultepec. Longstreet was a close friend to U. S. Grant before the Civil War and had served as best man at Grant's wedding. One of Lee's most steadfast commanders, Longstreet fought from Manassas to Appomattox with distinction.

By contrast, Jeb Stuart justifiably earned his reputation as a dashing, flamboyant cavalry leader and scourge of his Union adversaries. Just under six feet tall and powerfully built, Jeb's full beard and sparkling eyes set off his ruddy complexion. Stuart graduated from West Point in 1850, after which he served on the Texas frontier and in the Kansas Territory. Stuart had helped Lee capture John Brown at Harpers Ferry in 1859. As the "eyes" of Lee's army, he performed invaluable scouting and reconnaissance missions.

On June 8, Jeb Stuart invited Lee to review his cavalry at Brandy Station, a few miles northeast of Culpeper in the rolling piedmont (Atlantic plain) countryside.

General Jeb Stuart. *(Virginia Historical Society)*

Lee accepted and Stuart—colorfully uniformed in gray with brass buttons and braid, capped cavalierly with a plumed hat—put on a regal show with his ten thousand cavalrymen. Lee wrote Mary that Stuart "was in all his glory." The next day, the Yankees reminded Stuart that there was a war going on.

The battle of Brandy Station (June 9, 1863)—the largest purely cavalry battle of the war—erupted when a contingent of Union cavalry under Major General Alfred Pleasonton surprised Jeb Stuart's encampment. Stuart recovered from his surprise and rallied his horsemen. As his West Point classmate Dorsey Pender put it

W. H. F. "Rooney" Lee. *(Library of Congress)*

later, Stuart "retrieved the surprise by whipping them in the end." The battle actually ended in a tactical standoff. Pleasonton incurred more than nine hundred casualties out of twelve thousand men; Stuart, about five hundred of ten thousand.

Lee arrived at the battle site in time to see his son Rooney being carried to the rear with a bullet in his thigh. Rooney was sent to his wife's family home at Hickory Hill to recuperate. Lee found time to pen a note to Rooney's wife, Charlotte. "I am grieved, my dear daughter, to send Fitzhugh to you wounded," he wrote. "With his youth and strength to aid him, and your tender care to nurse him, I trust he will soon be well again." Rooney eventually recovered but never saw action again.

Meanwhile, as a result of the cavalry clash at Brandy Station, Hooker had learned of Lee's movements. Once he recognized that Lee was moving away from Fredericksburg, he proposed another advance on Richmond to force Lee to pull back his forces. But President Lincoln distrusted Hooker's judgment after his mishandling of the battle at Chancellorsville. He overruled his proposal and ordered him to follow Lee everywhere he went, keeping his army between Lee and Washington at all times. On June 14, Hooker wired Lincoln his assurance: "If the enemy should be making for Maryland, I will make the best dispositions in my power to come up with him."

That same day, in the Shenandoah Valley, Ewell's II Corps completed a rout of a Federal brigade under Major General Robert H. Milroy in the second battle of Winchester (June 13–14, 1863). Ewell killed or captured 4,443 Federals—a third of Milroy's command—while taking only 269 casualties himself. When news of the Winchester debacle reached Lincoln, he sent a curt wire to Hooker: "If the head of Lee's army is at Martinsburg and the tail of it on the Plank road between Fredericksburg and Chancellorsville, the animal must be very slim somewhere. Could you not break him?" But with his own army already stretching to track Lee, Hooker could do little at that moment.

Following Ewell's clearing action, Lee ordered Hill's corps out of Fredericksburg on June 14. His entire Army of Northern Virginia was now in motion and heading toward Union territory, screened by Jeb Stuart east of the Blue Ridge Mountains. After all three of Lee's corps had passed to the west of the mountains, an inspired notion struck Stuart, which he forwarded to Lee on June 22: Stuart figured he could screen Lee's movements with two of his cavalry brigades. This would enable him to move his other three brigades across the Potomac and harass Hooker's movements in one of his sweeping "ride-arounds" at the same time. On June 23, Lee replied, "If you find that he [the enemy] is moving northward, and that two brigades can guard the Blue Ridge & take care of your rear, you can move with the other three into Maryland & take up position on General Ewell's right, place yourself in communication with him, guard his flank, keep him informed of the enemy's movements & collect all the supplies you can for use of the [Confederate] army."

Stuart's message to Lee said nothing about another ride-around, and Lee's reply did not restrict Stuart to a specific itinerary. Thus, free to roam—and perhaps motivated by a desire to reestablish the superiority of his cavalry and restore his own reputation after his lapse at Brandy Station—Stuart chose once again to encircle the Army of the Potomac. This time, however, the Union army actively controlled far more territory than Stuart had supposed, and the Federals drove Stuart's raiders far to the east. Lee would not hear from Stuart, his main source of intelligence, for ten days.

With the avenue to the North cleared by Ewell's corps, Lee's Army of Northern Virginia moved unopposed across the Potomac River and into Pennsylvania. On June 27, while encamped along the way, Lee pointed to an area on his map around Gettysburg and suggested to a subordinate that it might provide the site of their next battle: "Our army is in good spirits, not overly fatigued,

At one point during Jeb Stuart's controversial diversion from Lee's army, he showed up in Carlisle, Pennsylvania, and, as portrayed here, skirmished with local militia before learning that Lee was engaged in heated battle in Gettysburg.

and can be concentrated on any point in twenty-four hours or less. I have not yet heard that the enemy have crossed the Potomac, and am waiting to hear from General Stuart. . . . They will come up, probably through Frederick, broken down with hunger and hard marching. . . . I shall throw an overwhelming force on their advance, crush it, follow up the success, [and] drive one corps back and another . . . create a panic and virtually destroy the army."

Lead elements of Lee's army passed through Chambersburg and arrived at Carlisle and York on June 28. Because of Jeb Stuart's impulsive decision to ride around Hooker's army, Lee now found himself operating in hostile territory without Stuart—his "eyes"—who was off marauding in Maryland. To anyone who might provide an answer, Lee constantly asked, "Can you tell where General Stuart is?" or "Where on earth is my cavalry?" As far as Lee knew, the Army of the Potomac was still south of the Potomac.

In the meantime, once Hooker had finally satisfied himself that Lee was making a major movement, he had commenced moving north with his army of one hundred fifteen thousand men on June 27. Along the way, he repeatedly missed chances to strike at Lee's stretched-out forces, continually complaining to Washington that Lee's army of seventy-five thousand outnumbered his own. Upon his arrival at Frederick, Maryland, Hooker learned that Washington had overruled his latest plan to trap Lee with a two-pronged strategic envelopment. Angry and frustrated, Hooker tendered his resignation to Washington, supremely confident that Lincoln and Halleck would not accept it. But they did.

Hooker's replacement, General George G. Meade. *(Library of Congress)*

On June 28, Halleck replaced Hooker with Major General George G. Meade, making Meade the fifth commander of the Army of the Potomac in ten months. Lee, despite a lack of intelligence resulting from Stuart's absence, learned of the general location of the Army of the Potomac and of Meade's ascension to command through a paid Confederate spy. Lee knew Meade as a friend from the old army. He was the kind of general not likely to make mistakes, Lee declared. "And if I make one," he added, "he will make haste to take advantage of it." The next day, Lee concentrated his forces near the little roadside town of Cashtown, Pennsylvania, nine miles west of Gettysburg. That afternoon, Lee told his officers, "Tomorrow, gentlemen, we will not move to Harrisburg, as we expected, but will go over to Gettysburg and see what General Meade is after."

On June 30, Meade started to probe cautiously toward Emmitsburg and Hanover, trying to coax Lee into giving battle south of the Susquehanna River. By chance, Major General John Buford's Union cavalry brigade reconnoitering northwest stumbled upon Brigadier General James J. Pettigrew's South Carolina infantry brigade moving southeast toward Gettysburg in search of shoes. The two forces clashed in what militarists define as a meeting engagement or an encounter battle—literally, a collision. In the next three days, this chance encounter escalated, step by step, into the greatest battle ever fought on American soil. That night, General Lee went to bed still wondering where Jeb Stuart was.

On July 1, the first day of the Battle of Gettysburg (July 1–3, 1863), neither side had reached the battle site with all its forces. Lee had told his corps commanders, "I am not prepared to bring on a general engagement today—Longstreet is not up." By the time Lee arrived at 2:00 PM, however, the engagement had "generally" commenced.

A. P. Hill's Confederate III Corps opposed Major General John F. Reynolds's Union I Corps and Major General Oliver O. Howard's XI Corps west and north of Gettysburg, respectively—twenty-four thousand Confederates facing nineteen thousand Federals. The Rebels drove the Yankees through the town in chaotic fighting. Meanwhile, Ewell's II Corps moved south from Heidlersburg and outflanked the Union right. The Federals managed to rally south of Gettysburg on two prominences known as Cemetery Hill and Culp's Hill, while the Confederates secured the town and lodged into positions on Seminary Ridge to the southwest.

Lee, after observing the unfolding action, sent staff member Walter H. Taylor to inform Ewell that he should take the heights. Lee, as usual, left the implementation of his order to his subordinate commander.

Longstreet joined Lee on Seminary Ridge later that afternoon. After studying the action, he offered Lee his considered opinion on the strategy called for by the situation:

> All we have to do is throw our army around by their left [south], and we shall interpose between the Federal army and Washington. We can get a strong position and wait, and if they fail to attack us we shall have everything in condition to move back tomorrow night in the direction of Washington, selecting beforehand a good position into which we can place our troops to

This painting, called "Attack at Seminary Ridge," depicts the bitter fighting of the first day of combat, which resulted in a Confederate victory, at Gettysburg. *(Museum of Fine Arts, Boston)*

receive battle the next day . . . the Federals will be sure to attack us. When they attack, we shall beat them, as we proposed to do before we left Fredericksburg, and the probabilities are that the fruits of our success will be great.

In short, Longstreet wanted to fight a defensive battle in Pennsylvania, similar to their hugely successful battles at Fredericksburg and Chancellorsville in Virginia. Lee pondered the advice of his subordinate and said, "No, the enemy is there, and I am going to attack him there." Lee still hoped to score that one great victory that would break the back, mind, and spirit of the Northerners. The first day's fighting ended with the Federals in severe jeopardy. Throughout the night, Meade marched up with the remainder of his Army of the Potomac and moved into position facing west along Cemetery Ridge, opposite Seminary Ridge. His line of deployment roughly formed the shape of a fishhook and stretched about four miles from its barb at Culp's Hill to the end of its shank at another hill to the south called Big Round Top. The "fishhook" has since emerged as an integral part of most accounts of the historic battle. That evening, Lee decided to envelop the Union left the next morning, utilizing Longstreet's corps, which still had not arrived on scene.

On day two of the battle, Longstreet's attack did not commence until afternoon for reasons still not fully explained. Although delayed, the attack of Longstreet's I Corps succeeded in driving back Major General Daniel E. Sickles's III Corps from an exposed bulge in the Union lines in a peach orchard west of Cemetery Ridge. Longstreet's Confederates tried valiantly to turn the Union left but fell narrowly short.

In the late afternoon, Brigadier General Gouverneur K. Warren, Meade's engineering officer, discovered that the hill called Little Round Top was unmanned at the

This painting shows an overview of the rolling countryside that was the landscape of the Battle of Gettysburg. *(Library of Congress)*

shank of the fishhook. He skillfully diverted a nearby Union brigade and artillery battery to the key prominence, thereby saving the southern anchor of the Union defense line from imminent disaster. Later, ferocious action on the hill featured Colonel Joshua L. Chamberlain and his 20th Maine Regiment defending against repeated thrusts by Colonel William C. Oates's 15th Alabama Regiment. Eventually, the troops from Maine ran out of ammunition, leaving Chamberlain with only one option. Recalling that moment years later, he wrote: "The men turned towards me. One word was enough— BAYONETS!"

The 20th Maine fixed bayonets and charged downhill, wrote their leader, "down into the face of half a thousand! Two hundred men!" Down they lunged, plunging cold steel into warm bodies in a frenzied killing foray, to save the hill called Little Round Top. When the red-tinged melee ended, as Oates recalled later, "The blood stood in puddles in some places on the rocks." And the 20th Maine still owned the hill.

Also that afternoon, Jeb Stuart and his cavalry rejoined Lee on Seminary Ridge. Lee said, "Well, General Stuart, you are here at last." That was all. Stuart had returned far too late to provide the intelligence that might have enabled Lee to forestall a major battle with Meade until a time and place of Lee's choosing. But, then, Meade was also surprised by the chance encounter that touched off the action.

The second day of desperate fighting ended with the

Federals anchored firmly along the ridge from Big Round Top to Culp's Hill. Ewell had failed to wrest the latter hill from Union hands. That night, Lee decided to launch a full-scale assault on the center of the Union lines the next day, aimed at penetrating Meade's defenses and driving him off the battlefield.

Lee named Longstreet to direct the attack, although two-thirds of the troops were of other commands, and Longstreet opposed Lee's attack strategy. Longstreet later wrote: "I thought that it would not do; that the point had been fully tested the day before, by more men, when all were fresh; that the enemy was there looking for us, as we heard him during the night putting up defences; . . . that thirty thousand men was the minimum force necessary for the work." But Lee could spare only fifteen thousand men for the task. Longstreet pointed out that those men "had never been arrayed for battle; but he was impatient of listening, and tired of talking, and nothing was left except to proceed." And proceed they did—tragically.

Again, the assault got started late. Commencing in mid-afternoon, following an enormous artillery bombardment, ten Confederate brigades stepped to the attack on the Union-held ridgeline. History records their assault as Pickett's Charge, although Major General George E. Pickett represented but one of four commanders who took part in the attack. Some 15,500 men charged for more than a mile through Union cannon fire that blasted great holes in their ranks. The resolute Confed-

In this portrayal of Longstreet giving Pickett his orders for the fateful charge, Longstreet seems to realize the potential for great loss and cannot even look Pickett in the eye. *(Library of Congress)*

erates broke through the Union defenses briefly only to be thrown back by equally determined Federal reserves. Only about half of the Confederates survived the assault. They reeled back to Seminary Ridge in battered disarray. When Lee directed Pickett to reassemble his division for a counterattack, Pickett replied, "General Lee, I have no division now."

Meanwhile, several brigades of Jeb Stuart's cavalry were heavily engaged with their Union counterparts. Stuart, attempting to ride to the right rear of the Federal army, was met by Union cavalry, including a Michigan brigade led by Brevet Brigadier General George A. Custer. The mounted enemies collided at a combined speed of fifty miles an hour. Medal of Honor winner Captain William E. Miller described their clash in the battle's aftermath: "The meeting was as the crash of ocean waves breaking upon a rock-bound coast, and men and horses rolled and tossed like foam upon its crest." At dusk, Stuart called off his cavalry and rejoined Lee's army. Lee settled in to await a Union counterattack. It never came.

The battle at Gettysburg cost Lee's army over twenty-eight thousand troops killed, wounded, and missing. Meade's losses totaled over twenty-three thousand. When the slaughter ended, Lee accepted full responsibility for the carnage. That night, while discussing his imminent retreat with Brigadier General John D. Imboden, Lee said, "I never saw troops behave more magnificently than Pickett's division of Virginians did today in that grand charge upon the enemy. And if they had been supported as they were to have been—but, for some reason not yet fully explained to me, were not—we would have held the position [during the Confederate breakthrough

The carnage at Gettysburg was captured in dozens of startling photographs by Matthew Brady. This one, taken only hours after the battle, shows heaps of Confederate dead at the foot of Little Round Top. *(Library of Congress)*

on Cemetery Ridge] and the day would have been ours."

Lee paused for a moment, then added in an uncharacteristically loud voice, "Too bad! *Too bad! OH TOO BAD!"* In his comment about a lack of support, Lee was referring to a failure of his units to achieve a simultaneous attack on the entire Union line. Some military analysts attribute the lapse to Longstreet's delay in positioning his troops for attack, but to this day the subject is one of heated controversy.

While Lee was suffering his greatest loss in the East, the Confederate stronghold at Vicksburg surrendered with thirty thousand troops to Ulysses S. Grant on July 4, 1863, opening up the Mississippi River to the Union and shutting off a major source of Confederate supplies. The war would continue for almost two more years, but for the South it was all but over.

During the next eleven days (July 4–14), despite rain, mud, and a swollen Potomac, Lee withdrew back to Virginia without serious hindrance from Meade's battered army. Meade followed along cautiously but failed to exploit his advantage, much to President Lincoln's grave disappointment.

9

Retreat, Siege, and Surrender

Following Lee's defeat at Gettysburg—by most estimates his worst battle—Lee was forced to abandon his strategic philosophy of offensive defense. With his army growing smaller by the day, and with essential materials and food supplies diminishing rapidly, he had little choice but to settle for a defensive war. If the South could hold out long enough to erode Union morale, an honorable end to the fighting might yet be achieved through negotiation. For the moment, he could seek solace in knowing he had severely wounded Meade's army.

After Gettysburg, Lee told one of his officers that "it will be seen for the next six months that *that army* will be as quiet as a sucking dove." Actually, except for indecisive campaigns at Bristoe Station and Mine Run in October and November 1863, the Army of the Potomac would not launch another major offensive in Virginia until the next spring. Until then, Lee and his army—minus Longstreet's I Corps, which had been temporarily detached in September to reinforce General Braxton Bragg's Army of Tennessee—would lay in at his winter quarters on the Rapidan River.

Lee spent most of the winter of 1863–64 trying to feed and equip his army, which was barely existing on short rations and was plagued with desertions. On January 22, 1864, he wrote Confederate secretary of war James A. Seddon: "Unless there is a change, I fear the army cannot be kept together." Nevertheless, the Army of Northern Virginia held together, largely because of Lee's determination and ability to direct limited Confed-

A sentry stands guard at Lee's winter camp along the Rapidan River.

erate resources to it. His efforts to sustain his army came at a time when angina pectoris made physical exertion of any kind most painful. (Angina pectoris is a disease caused by a deficiency of oxygen in the heart

Mrs. Mary Custis Lee.

muscles and is marked by chest pains.) Although keeping his army intact required most of his time, he still managed to visit his wife on brief trips to Richmond.

Mary's health had declined precipitously, and she was now totally invalided. Lee found little in the news of his family to relieve the burden of high command. Custis, who was assigned to staff duty in Richmond, was looking after his mother, and the surviving daughters were with her. (Annie, Lee's oldest daughter, had contracted typhoid fever in North Carolina and had succumbed to it on October 20, 1862, at age twenty-three.) Rooney, who had been captured by the Federals while recuperating at Hickory Hill, remained a prisoner of war. Rooney's wife Charlotte, one of Lee's favorites, died of tuberculosis at the end of 1863, without getting to see her husband again. Young Rob was now in the army and off serving under his cousin Fitzhugh.

Beyond question, the last half of 1863 had tested the limit of Lee's unshakable faith in a merciful Providence. And the god of war was preparing even greater tests for the year ahead. In early March 1864, President Abraham Lincoln summoned Ulysses S. Grant to Washington, promoted him to lieutenant general, and appointed him general in chief of all Federal armies. To clear the way for Grant, Lincoln kicked Halleck upstairs to the newly created post of chief of staff. The war was about to grow grim for the South.

Grant was a fighting general. He came to Washington after compiling a string of impressive victories in the

General Ulysses S. Grant. *(West Point Museum)*

West, at Forts Henry and Donelson and Shiloh, in Tennessee; at Iuka and Vicksburg, in Mississippi; and in Tennessee again to lift the Confederate siege of Chattanooga. After a succession of disappointing confrontations with "Bobby" Lee in the East, Lincoln wanted a general who would fight Lee to the death. Grant was his man. In his first meeting with the president, Grant told Lincoln, "With the aid of the noble armies that have fought in so many fields for our common country, it will be my earnest endeavor not to disappoint your expectations."

Grant set to work at once preparing a grand campaign against Lee. He kept Meade as commander of the Army of the Potomac, approved Meade's plan for reorganizing the army for maximum effectiveness, and summoned Major General Philip H. Sheridan, a tough infantry officer from the Army of the Cumberland, and put him in charge of Meade's cavalry. Not content to direct his campaign from behind a desk in Washington, Grant established his headquarters with the Army of the Potomac in the field. Although Meade remained in command of the army, Grant would exercise so much control over it that people would speak of it as Grant's army in the days ahead.

Grant joined Meade at his camp in the general vicinity of Culpeper Courthouse, a few miles south of where the Army of the Potomac had been camped at the start of the war. Grant's strategy was simple: destroy the enemy on all fronts. Grant's plan called for Meade's army to drive toward Richmond while Major General William T. Sherman's army advanced on Atlanta. At the same time, Major General Benjamin F. Butler's Army of the James was to move up the south bank of the James River toward Richmond, while a small Union army under German-born Major General Franz Sigel in the

Shenandoah Valley moved through the Blue Ridge Mountains and pressed on toward the Confederate capital. All four armies would move in unison, occasioned by the movement of Meade's army. For the first time in the war, the Union armies, under Grant, were preparing to open a synchronized campaign on all fronts under central control.

In April, while Grant prepared to move against the Army of Northern Virginia, Lee welcomed back Longstreet and his I Corps from eastern Tennessee in an emotional review of the troops. One observer on the scene recalled later that "a wild and prolonged cheer, fraught with a feeling that thrilled all hearts, ran along the lines and rose to the heavens." Longstreet's return boosted Lee's ranks to about sixty-five thousand men, who were soon to face a Federal army of some one hundred twenty thousand troops.

Grant began his Overland campaign—major battles followed by lesser skirmishes, followed by major battles and then more of the same—against Lee in early May 1864. In the battle of the Wilderness (May 4–7), in the same snarled thicket of pines and scrub oaks in which Stonewall Jackson had surprised Fighting Joe Hooker at Chancellorsville, Grant tried and failed to outflank Lee. In the close quarters of the forest, Longstreet was wounded in the leg with a minié ball, a muzzle-loading rifle bullet with a conical head. Just as Jackson had in an earlier encounter in the Wilderness, Longstreet fell victim to friendly fire. Hard fighting and forest fires claimed nearly eighteen thousand Federal casualties, against unrecorded Confederate casualties estimated at more than twelve thousand.

Of Grant's assault on Lee in the Wilderness, and of Grant's subsequent campaign in Virginia, Walter H. Taylor, the adjutant general of Lee's army, later wrote:

> General Grant earned the title of a great commander; but his is not the brightest name that emerges from the smoke of battle at that eventful period, for higher yet in the Temple of Fame will be found the name of him who, though greatly outnumbered, held his adversary at bay for nearly a year, checked his every move, repulsed his every attack, and only gave up the struggle from a sense of duty to his men, when his army had been reduced to but a shadow of its former self by incessant contact with the enemy, whose losses were constantly recouped, and whose numerical strength was unimpaired.

The name in the "Temple of Fame," so eloquently referred to by Adjutant General Taylor, was, of course, that of his commander, Robert E. Lee.

Undeterred by his failure to outflank Lee in the Wilderness, Grant continued to push south. Lee, anticipating his movements and maneuvering skillfully, rushed his forces to Spotsylvania Courthouse, where he built up his position in an enormous V, with its apex—called the "Bloody Angle"—pointing north. When Grant arrived, he went after the most prominent part of the line and the battle of Spotsylvania (May 8–19) erupted. When Grant found no weaknesses in the V, he probed and failed to find Lee's flank. After eleven days of fighting, the battle finally petered out. Grant had over fourteen thousand casualties; Lee, more than ten thousand.

While Lee struggled with Grant at Spotsylvania, Phil Sheridan and his ten thousand-man cavalry corps raided Yellow Tavern, near Richmond, and dealt Lee a stunning blow. Jeb Stuart's cavalry engaged Sheridan's horsemen on the outskirts of the town. Stuart had once vowed, "I had rather die than be whipped." Sheridan drove the Confederates from the field, inflicting about one thousand casualties on Stuart's cavaliers while taking four hundred of his own. Stuart took a .44-caliber bullet in his right side below his ribs and died in bed on May 12.

On hearing of Stuart's passing, Lee said, "I can scarcely think of him without weeping." But in a revealing note to himself he wrote: "The warmest instincts of every man's soul declare the glory of the soldier's death."

Meanwhile, P. G. T. Beauregard rebuffed Ben Butler's effort to advance on Petersburg in the battle of Drewry's Bluff (May 15) and sent him scurrying back to Bermuda Hundred Landing, south of the James River. Butler remained bottled up there until Grant crossed the river. On that same day, Major General John C. Breckinridge halted the advance of Franz Sigel's Federals in the Shenandoah Valley with a victory in the battle of New Market.

Lee, anticipating Grant's movements, continued to

stay a step ahead of him. From May 23 to June 1, he repulsed Grant's advances at the North Anna River and then moved south to take up a strong defensive position at Cold Harbor, near the site of Lee's earlier victories in the Seven Days campaign. A Northern journalist described Lee's entrenchments as "intricate, zig-zagged lines within lines, lines protecting flanks of lines . . . a maze and labyrinth of works within works and works without works."

Grant, determined to crush Lee's defenses in the battle of Cold Harbor (June 3-12), ordered a frontal assault on the "labyrinth of works." The result was pure butchery. A Federal from New Hampshire wrote: "It was undoubtedly the greatest and most inexcusable slaughter of the whole war. . . . The men went down in rows, just as they marched in ranks, and so many at a time that

In his memoirs, Grant confided, "I have always regretted that the last assault at Cold Harbor was ever made. . . . No advantage whatever was gained to compensate for the heavy loss we sustained." *(Library of Congress)*

those in the rear of them thought they were lying down." Confederate defenders mowed down more than seven thousand Federal attackers in less than an hour. Brigadier General Evander M. Law, commander of an Alabama brigade in the action, summed up the carnage in D. H. Hill's often-cited sentence: "It was not war, it was murder." Federal losses in the ten-day battle totaled more than thirteen thousand; Confederate losses, about three thousand.

Right after Cold Harbor, Lee confided his deepest fear to Jubal Early. "We must destroy this army of Grant's before he gets to [the] James River," he said. "[I]f he gets there, it will become a siege, and then it will become a mere question of time." Grant then did the unexpected: fooling Lee completely, he pulled away from the Confederates at Cold Harbor, crossed the James River, and hastened toward Petersburg, twenty-three miles south of Richmond. The scenario Lee dreaded most was starting to materialize.

Grant ordered Ben Butler and his Army of the James to march on Petersburg and secure it while it was scantily garrisoned, but Butler and his subordinate W. F. Smith botched the job in two piecemeal assaults on the city. Lee rushed reinforcements to Petersburg and joined P. G. T. Beauregard in the defense of the city. When Grant arrived with the bulk of the Union army, some forty thousand Confederates staved off about sixty-five thousand Federals in the battle of Petersburg (June 15–18). Unable to breach Lee's defenses, Grant laid siege to the city and ended his Overland campaign. In just over a month, Grant had lost over sixty thousand men. Lee's smaller army had also been halved.

Grant's siege of Petersburg dragged on for more than nine months. Lee used the time to construct a maze of defensive works along the Petersburg-Richmond line, while Grant continued to expand his lines westward in an effort to turn Lee's flank. Once in a while, sharp actions broke the monotony of static warfare. Lee ordered his last diversion, sending the irascible but highly capable Jubal Early into the Shenandoah Valley. After Early prevailed in a few minor actions, Grant sent Phil Sheridan to destroy Early's command. He told Sheridan to "eat out Virginia clean and clear . . . so that crows flying over it for the balance of the season will have to carry their own provender [feed]." Sheridan eventually defeated Early in the Shenandoah Valley campaign (September–October 1864), but not before the Confederate leader had extended the war in the East by about six months.

Meanwhile, William T. Sherman's Union army occupied Atlanta on September 3, helping Abraham Lincoln's bid for a second term as president. Lincoln's reelection in November 1864 ended Southern hopes that a change of administrations in Washington might open the door to a negotiated peace. Lee wrote Mary: "We must therefore make up our minds for another four years of war." Considering the desperate plight of the South at that time, any suggestion that the Confederacy could possi-

Sherman's occupying Federal camps in the heart of Atlanta on Decatur Street. *(Library of Congress)*

bly sustain a war for four more years sounds disingenuous at best. Only three months later, Lee would propose to the Confederate Congress the enlistment of slaves as a means of keeping an army in the field: "The negroes, under proper circumstances, will make efficient soldiers. . . . Those who are [so] employed should be freed. It would be neither just nor wise . . . to require them to serve as slaves."

On February 6, the Confederate Congress appointed Lee general in chief of all Confederate forces. To Lee, the appointment represented a meaningless gesture aimed at giving heart to the army he was struggling to hold together. Five weeks later on March 13, 1865, Congress voted to enlist blacks for service but did not provide for freeing those who served. Two companies of blacks were enlisted, neither of which saw any action.

As the end of March 1865 drew near, it was becoming obvious the war was over. Lee launched a last frantic effort to break Grant's siege at Petersburg with an attack on Fort Stedman on March 25. Lee's assault achieved momentary success, but counterattacking Federals took back their lost position. A week later, Phil Sheridan crushed George E. Pickett's defenders at the battle of Five Forks (April 1), exposing the entire right of Lee's lines and forcing Lee to evacuate Richmond on the night of April 2–3. Meanwhile, Grant breached Lee's defenses at Petersburg. A. P. Hill, another of Lee's trusted lieutenants, was killed.

Pursued by a human tide of Union soldiers, Lee and the diminishing Army of Northern Virginia streaked westward, attempting to reach Amelia Courthouse where Lee hoped to find rations to feed his starving troops. With food under their belts, his soldiers might still find the strength and will to move south and link up with Joseph E. Johnston's forces, who were then battling Sherman's Federals in the Carolinas. But Lee found no food at Amelia Courthouse, and Grant cut off the foraging Confederates at Sayler's Creek on April 6.

Three Federal corps found a gap in Lee's lines and attacked, killing—but mostly capturing—some eight thousand graycoats. Lee, while observing the disordered remainder of one of his corps from the crest of a hill, exclaimed, "My God! has the army been dissolved?" His once-powerful army now numbered just ten thousand.

On Sunday, April 9, 1865, hemmed in by Federal forces to the south, east, and west, Lee recognized that the end had come at last. To a gathering of his officers, he said, "Then there is nothing left me but to go and see General Grant, and I would rather die a thousand deaths." Lee arranged to meet with Grant that afternoon at the home of Wilmer McLean in the Appomattox Courthouse.

At midday, Lee rode out to Appomattox Courthouse on his Confederate-gray horse, Traveller, accompanied by his aide Colonel Charles Marshall and an orderly bearing a flag of truce. En route to his meeting with Grant, Lee passed between the lines of Joshua Chamberlain. The Union hero of Little Round Top heard a commotion behind him and, as he noted later, "I turned about, and there behind me . . . appeared a commanding form, superbly mounted, richly accoutered [with a full-dress uniform and a borrowed ceremonial sword], of imposing bearing, noble countenance, with an expression of deep sadness overmastered by deeper strength. It is none other than Robert E. Lee! . . . I sat immovable, with a certain awe and inspiration."

Lee arrived at the McLean house ahead of Grant, dismounted, and went in. Grant, having ridden the far-

Lee surrendering to Grant at the McLean House at Appomattox Courthouse *(Jo Daviess County History Museum, Virginia)*

thest, joined him a half-hour later, dressed in a mud-splattered, dark blue tunic. He wore riding boots but no spurs, belt, or sword. The two most famous generals of the Civil War reminisced briefly about their mutual experiences during the Mexican War until Lee turned the conversation to the purpose of their meeting. Lee first asked that his troops be fed. They were. Grant then offered Lee generous surrender terms. Lee surrendered his army but not his sword.

The meeting was brief and conducted with solemnity and grace. When it ended, Lee strode to the front porch and called, "Orderly! Orderly!" His orderly brought around Traveller. Lee mounted and as he was riding off, Grant appeared on the front porch and removed his hat. Others followed suit. Lee tipped his own hat and was gone.

Lee rejoined his troops. They were eating. Their white-haired commander simply said, "Men, we have fought through the war together; I have done my best for you; my heart is too full to say more." Lee walked into an orchard by himself and paced. Many of his gray-clad soldiers wept.

Afterward, Lee assigned a staff officer to write his farewell address to his troops, for which he provided eloquent requirements. Unit commanders read it later to what was left of their units. It stated, in part:

> After four years of arduous service, marked by unsurpassed courage and fortitude, the Army of Northern Virginia has been compelled to yield to overwhelming numbers and resources. . . . By the terms of the agreement, officers and men can return to their homes, and remain there until exchanged. You will take with you the satisfaction that proceeds from the consciousness of duty faithfully performed; and I earnestly pray that a merciful God will extend to you his blessing and protection. With an increasing admiration of your constancy and devotion to your country, and a grateful remembrance of your kind and generous consideration of myself, I bid you an affectionate farewell.

Confederate forces outside Virginia surrendered in May, and the bloodiest war in American history ended. After almost thirty-six years in the service of his country and his conscience, General Robert E. Lee now found himself without a home or job, nearly penniless, in failing health, and facing an uncertain future. If such vicissitudes were not sufficient to cast a pall over what lay ahead for Lee, the government of the United States added an indictment for treason.

Shortly after the war ended, U. S. Grant interceded on Lee's behalf with President Andrew Johnson over Lee's indictment for treason. Grant told his former antagonist

This photograph of Lee was taken by Matthew Brady just after the surrender. *(Library of Congress)*

he would not be prosecuted, but the charge against Lee was not dropped formally until 1869. On June 13, 1865, Lee signed and submitted an amnesty oath in the hope of regaining his U.S. citizenship. Secretary of State William H. Seward, without granting Lee the courtesy of a response, gave Lee's oath to a friend as a souvenir. Lee did not regain full U.S. citizenship until President Gerald Ford restored it in 1975.

In August 1865, the board of trustees of Washington

College, in Lexington, Virginia, unanimously elected Lee as president of the college. Lee accepted the position, saying, "I think it is the duty of every citizen, in the present condition of the Country, to do all in his power to aid in the restoration of peace and harmony. . . . It is particularly incumbent upon those charged with the instruction of the young to set them an example of submission to authority."

Duty called, as it had so many times in his life, and Lee answered its call. In the time remaining to him, he became a very good educator, helping to shape the school curriculum and adding such classes as postclassical literature, law, and journalism.

Lee mentored an enrollment of twenty-five young men like a doting father. It was perhaps his way of repaying thousands of other young men who had given their all for him. On one occasion, a student who had been endangering his health by long hours of overwork on his studies explained that he was "impatient to make up for the time I lost in the army." Lee turned red of face and admonished the young man. "Mr. Humphreys!" he said. "However long you live and whatever you accomplish, you will find that the time you spent in the Confederate army was the most profitably spent portion of your life." In his heart, Lee may have shared the youth's feeling, for time was fast running out for him.

In March 1870, no longer young at age sixty-three and weakening with what is now called arteriosclerosis (abnormal thickening and hardening of the arteries),

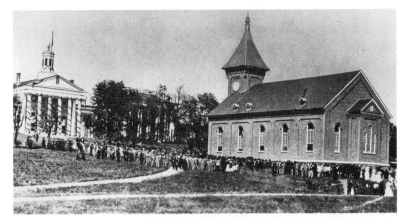

Lee's funeral at Washington and Lee in Lexington, VA. Soldiers from the nearby Virginia Military Institute came to carry Lee's coffin.

Lee took two months off to visit his daughter Annie's grave in North Carolina. Later, after a Baltimore doctor incorrectly diagnosed his condition as related to rheumatism, Lee spent the following July and August at health resorts. He wrote Mary Lee: "I hope that I am better, but am aware of no material change, except that I am weaker." He returned home in September.

On September 27, after presiding over a three-hour vestry meeting, Lee suffered a stroke at the family dinner table while attempting to say grace. The Confederate icon lingered in a torpor until the morning of October 12, 1870. His doctors later reported: "Soon after 9 o'clock AM he turned, with assistance, upon his right side, then closed his eyes and as tranquilly as the setting sun his noble spirit passed into the presence of his Maker." Robert Edward Lee—the first soldier of the Confederacy—was dead.

General Robert E. Lee is buried with other members of his family beneath the chapel on the campus of Washington and Lee University.

Timeline

1807 Born on January 19 at Stratford Hall.

1811 Moves to Alexandria, Virginia, with his family.

1818 Father dies at Cumberland Island, Georgia, on March 25.

1825 Enters U.S. Military Academy at West Point.

1829 Graduates from West Point. Mother dies on July 10.

1831 Marries Mary Custis of Arlington, Virginia, on June 30.

1836- Assigned to various engineering duties; appointed to
1846 board of visitors at West Point.

1846 Renders two years of service in the Mexican War.

1852 Serves as superintendent at West Point until 1855.

1859 Quells John Brown's uprising at Harpers Ferry.

1861 Resigns commission in the U.S. Army after Virginia secedes from the Union. Accepts command of Virginia forces with the rank of major general.

1862 Assumes command of the Confederate Army of Northern Virginia. Fights Seven Days campaign and battles of second Bull Run, Antietam, and Fredericksburg.

1863 Fights battles at Chancellorsville and Gettysburg.

1864 Fights battles at Spotsylvania, Cold Harbor; siege of Petersburg begins.

1865 Retreats from Petersburg; Richmond falls; surrenders the Army of Northern Virginia to Grant at Appomattox Courthouse, Virginia. Elected president of Washington College (now Washington and Lee University).

1870 Dies in Lexington, Virginia on October 12.

Sources

CHAPTER ONE: Prospects

p. 9, "First in war . . ." J. Steven Wilkins, *Call of Duty: The Sterling Nobility of Robert E. Lee,* Leaders in Action series (Nashville, TN: Cumberland House Publishing, 1997), 33.

p. 11, "promises the most . . ." Emory M. Thomas, *Robert E. Lee: A Biography* (New York: W. W. Norton, 1997), 24.

p. 11, "became [Lee's] delighted wife . . ." Ibid., 26.

p. 12, "free from the claim . . ." Roy Blount Jr., *Robert E. Lee,* A Penguin Life series (New York: Viking, 2003), 17.

p. 12, "much of an invalid . . ." Thomas, *Robert E. Lee*, 28.

p. 14, "I feel an unconquerable . . ." Ibid., 31.

CHAPTER TWO: The Marble Model

p. 15, "one of the finest women . . ." Robert R. Brown, *"And One Was a Soldier": The Spiritual Pilgrimage of Robert E. Lee* (Shippensburg, PA: White Mane Books, 1998), 4.

p. 15, "we had a large family . . ." Paul C. Nagel, *The Lees of Virginia: Seven Generations of an American Family* (New York: Oxford University Press, 1990), 198.

p. 18, "base villains," Blount, *Robert E. Lee*, 15.

p. 19, "We have very seldom . . ." Thomas, *Robert E. Lee*, 16.

p. 19-20, "Robert was always . . ." Ibid., 34.

p. 20, "Whip and pray . . ." John M. Taylor, *Duty Faithfully Performed: Robert E. Lee and His Critics* (Dulles, VA:

Brassey's, 2000), 14.

p. 20-21, "to practice self-denial . . ." Wilkins, *Call of Duty*, 41.

p. 22, "His name might be . . ." Rod Gragg, comp. and ed. *A Commitment to Valor: A Character Portrait of Robert E. Lee* (Nashville, TN: Rutledge Hill Press, 2001), 32.

p. 22, "I cannot consent to place . . ." Ibid., 90.

p. 23, "Self-command . . ." Wilkins, *Call of Duty*, 36.

p. 23, "Avoid debt . . ." Ibid., 37.

p. 24, "Duty . . . is the sublimest . . ." Bil Holton, *Leadership Lessons of Robert E. Lee: Tips, Tactics, and Strategies for Leaders and Managers* (New York: Gramercy Books, 1999), 38.

p. 25, "In the various branches . . ." Clifford Dowdey, *Lee* (Gettysburg, PA: Stan Clark Military Books, 1991), 41.

p. 26, "His specialty was . . ." Ibid., 42.

p. 29, "No other youth . . ." Taylor, *Duty Faithfully Performed*, 17.

p. 29, "I doubt if he ever . . ." Dowdey, *Lee*, 46.

CHAPTER THREE: Test of a Soldier

p. 31, "It seems now . . ." Dowdey, *Lee*, 47.

p. 32-33, "by the middle of November . . ." Douglas Southall Freeman, *Lee,* An abridgment in one volume by Richard Harwell of the four-volume *R. E. Lee* (New York: Simon & Schuster, 1997), 22.

p. 34, "I am engaged. . . ." Taylor, *Duty Faithfully Performed*, 22.

p. 36, "had few words to say . . ." Wilkins, *Call of Duty*, 50.

p. 38, "Although she was never awed . . ." Ibid., 51.

p. 38, "rather stupid," Taylor, *Duty Faithfully Performed*, 22.

p. 39, "Robert reads . . ." Ibid., 23.

p. 40, "tender and affectionate," Ibid., 25.

p. 40, "in favor of the pretty . . ." Thomas, *Robert E. Lee,* 73.

p. 40, "in the eyes of the world . . ." Thomas L. Connelly, *The Marble Man: Robert E. Lee and His Image in American Society* (Baton Rouge: Louisiana State University Press, 1978), 171.

p. 41, "fell upon the brain . . ." Thomas, *Robert E. Lee,* 84.

p. 42, "the duties of the office," Ibid., 75.

p. 43, "marvelously of Bilious . . ." Ibid., 82.

p. 43, "[W]hy do you . . ." Blount, *Robert E. Lee,* 34.

p. 44, "day by day in the hot . . ." Freeman, *Lee,* 42.

p. 46, "formed a charming portion . . ." Dowdey, *Lee,* 75.

p. 48, "In the event of war . . ." Thomas, *Robert E. Lee,* 111.

CHAPTER FOUR: Lessons in the Art of War

p. 50, "hostilities may now . . ." Robert Leckie, *The Wars of America* Vol. I. Updated Edition (New York: HarperCollins, 1993), 327.

p. 51, "After reiterated menaces . . ." Robert A. Rosenbaum, *The Penguin Encyclopedia of American History* (New York: Penguin Reference, 2003), 227.

p. 52-53, "to overspread and to possess . . ." Ibid., 219.

p. 53, "I have been very anxious . . ." Thomas, *Robert E. Lee,* 111.

p. 54, "It is the first time . . ." Dowdey, *Lee,* 80.

p. 55, "Of the officers of engineers . . ." Ibid.

p. 55, "History will record . . ." Wilkins, *Call of Duty,* 61.

p. 56, "[M]y poor Joe is so sick . . ." Thomas, *Robert E. Lee,* 119.

p. 56, "sink all the . . ." Leckie, *The Wars of America,* 355.

p. 58, "No matter where I turned . . ." Thomas, *Robert E. Lee,* 122.

p. 58, "isolated by rank or position . . ." Freeman, *Lee,* 59.

p. 61, "I am impelled to make . . ." Blount, *Robert E. Lee,* 46.

p. 62, "the gallant, indefatigable Captain . . ." Ibid., 47.

p. 63, "could no longer keep . . ." Thomas, *Robert E. Lee,* 136.

p. 64, "the very best soldier . . ." Ibid., 140.

p. 64, "almost idolatrous fancy . . ." Dowdey, *Lee,* 91.

p. 64, "Fighting is the easiest . . ." Taylor, *Duty Faithfully Performed,* 30.

CHAPTER FIVE: Lee's Choice

p. 66, "He came from Mexico . . ." *Robert Edward Lee* (Biography taken from the Confederate Military History, Volume I), http://www.civilwarhome.com/CMHLee.htm, 2.

p. 67, "perfectly surrounded by Mary . . ." Thomas, *Robert E. Lee,* 143.

p. 67, "Man's nature is so . . ." Taylor, *Duty Faithfully Performed,* 34.

p. 68, "I learn with much regret . . ." Freeman, *Lee,* 82.

p. 69, "Take them as you . . ." Thomas, *Robert E. Lee,* 152.

p. 70, "eminent qualifications . . ." Ibid., 161.

p. 70, "She was to me all . . ." Dowdey, *Lee,* 102.

p. 71, "The change from my present . . ." Ibid., 103.

p. 71, "You have often . . ." Taylor, *Duty Faithfully Performed,* 33–34.

p. 72, "the son of Light-Horse Harry Lee . . ." Blount, *Robert E. Lee,* 53.

p. 72, "the most barren . . ." Ibid., 54.

p. 75, "On arriving here . . ." Ibid., 66–67.

p. 76, "Lieutenant [Isaac] Green. . ." Ibid., 68.

p. 76, "Never mind us . . ." Wilkins, *Call of Duty,* 75.

p. 76, "The old revolutionary . . ." Ibid.

p. 77, "the attempt of a fanatic . . ." Thomas, *Robert E. Lee,* 183.

p. 78, "In this enlightened age . . ." Taylor, *Duty Faithfully Performed,* 40.

p. 78, "The blacks are . . ." Ibid.

p. 79, "If the slaves of the South . . ." Wilkins, *Call of Duty,* 297.

p. 81-82, "I can anticipate no greater . . ." Taylor, *Duty Faithfully Performed,* 46.

p. 84, "My husband was . . ." Dowdey, *Lee,* 129–130.

p. 84, "there needs to be no bloodshed . . ." George Childs Kohn, *Dictionary of Historic Documents,* rev. ed. (New York: Facts On File, 2003), 252.

p. 86, "stating as candidly . . ." Freeman, *Lee,* 110.

p. 86, "Lee, you have made . . ." Ibid.

CHAPTER SIX: A Shot for the Southern Cause

p. 87-88, "There are times . . ." Freeman, *Lee,* 110.

p. 88, "I have the honor to tender . . ." Ibid., 111.

p. 89, "more than 30 years . . ." Dowdey, *Lee,* 134.

p. 89, "Well, Mary, the question is . . ." Thomas, *Robert E. Lee,* 188.

p. 89, "the military and naval forces . . ." Ibid., 189.

p. 90, "No earthly act . . ." *Lee,* http://www.civilwarhome.com/ CMHLee.htm, 3.

p. 91, "Northern soldiers who profess . . ." Thomas, *Robert E. Lee,* 230.

p. 93, "Admirably proportioned . . ." Ibid., 192.

p. 94, "glorious victory . . ." Taylor, *Duty Faithfully Performed,* 55–56.

p. 94-95, "Sorrow for those . . ." Ibid., 56.

p. 95, "I wished to partake . . ." Blount, *Robert E. Lee,* 81.

p. 96, "a general who had . . ." Thomas, *Robert E. Lee,* 209.

p. 97, "I find it impossible . . ." Ibid., 213.

p. 97, "marked by a plain . . ." Taylor, *Duty Faithfully Performed,* 59.

p. 98, "If I were an artist . . ." Ibid.

p. 100, "The shot that struck . . ." Ibid., 66.

CHAPTER SEVEN: *Annus Mirabilis*

p. 103, "change the character . . ." Taylor, *Duty Faithfully Performed,* 70.

p. 103, "It will require 100,000 men . . ." Ibid.

p. 103, "spades & shovels being . . ." Ibid., 68.

p. 104, "I have determined to make . . ." Thomas, *Robert E. Lee,* 235.

p. 106, "It was not war . . ." Ibid., 243.

p. 108, "Our success has not . . ." Ibid.

p. 108, "Under ordinary circumstances . . ." Ibid.

p. 108, "No captain that ever lived . . ." Taylor, *Duty Faithfully Performed,* 78.

p. 109, "I must now leave the matter . . ." Ibid., 83.

p. 110-111, "so near and so thick . . ." Gary W. Gallagher, *The American Civil War: The war in the East 1861–May 1863,* Essential Histories series (Oxford, UK: Osprey Publishing, 2001), 46.

p. 111, "I saw the men . . ." Ibid.

p. 112, "get off without . . ." Ibid., 49.

p. 112, "Here is a paper with which . . ." James M. McPherson, *The Illustrated Battle Cry of Freedom: The Civil War Era* (New York: Oxford University Press, 2003), 461.

p. 113-114, "The truth is, when bullets . . ." Ibid., 464.

p. 114, "It is beyond all wonder . . ." Ibid.

p. 117, "It is well that war . . ." Wilkins, *Call of Duty,* 98.

p. 119, "They suffered heavily . . ." Gary W. Gallagher, "Robert E. Lee," in *Encyclopedia of the American Civil War: A Political, Social, and Military History,* Edited by David S. Heidler and Jeanne T. Heidler (New York: W. W. Norton, 2000), 1158.

p. 119, "If there is a worse place . . ." Ibid.

p. 119, "He is cheerful . . ." Ibid.

p. 121, "At Chancellorsville . . ." Ibid., 1159.

p. 122, "will take its own time . . ." Ibid.

CHAPTER EIGHT: Lee's Worst Battle

p. 125, "was in all his glory," Shelby Foote and the Editors of Time-Life Books. *The Civil War: A Narrative,* vol. 7, *Gettysburg to the Draft Riots.* 40th Anniv. Ed. (Alexandria, VA: Time-Life Books, 1999), 21.

p. 126, "retrieved the surprise . . ." Douglas Southall Freeman, *Lee's Lieutenants: A Study in Command.* Abridged in one volume by Stephen W. Sears (New York: Scribner, 1998), 540.

p. 126, "I am grieved, my dear . . ." Taylor, *Duty Faithfully Performed,* 135.

p. 127, "If the enemy should . . ." Foote, *The Civil War,* 35.

p. 127, "If the head of Lee's army . . ." Ibid.

p. 128, "If you find that he . . ." Craig L. Symonds, *Gettysburg: A Battlefield Atlas* (Baltimore, MD: Nautical & Aviation Publishing, 1992), 21.

p. 128-129, "Our army is in . . ." Taylor, *Duty Faithfully Performed,* 140.

p. 129, "Can you tell where . . ." Foote, *The Civil War,* 44.

p. 131, "And if I make one . . ." Dowdey, *Lee,* 364.

p. 131, "Tomorrow, gentlemen . . ." Leckie, *The Wars of America,* 469.

p. 131-132, "I am not prepared . . ." Thomas, *Robert E. Lee,* 295.

p. 132-133, "All we have to do . . ." Ibid., 295–296.

p. 133, "No, the enemy is there . . ." Ibid., 296.

p. 135, "The men turned. . . ." Joshua Lawrence Chamberlain, *Through Blood & Fire at Gettysburg: General Joshua Chamberlain and the 20th Maine* (Gettysburg, PA: Stan

Clark Military Books, 1994), 23.

p. 135, "down into the face of half . . ." Ibid.

p. 135, "The blood stood . . ." Foote, *The Civil War,* 107.

p. 135, "Well, General Stuart . . ." Emory M. Thomas, *Bold Dragoon: The Life of J.E.B. Stuart* (Norman: University of Oklahoma Press, 1999), 246.

p. 136, "I thought that it . . ." James Longstreet, *From Manassas to Appomattox: Memoirs of the Civil War in America* (Cambridge, MA: Da Capo Press, 1992), 386.

p. 136, "had never been arrayed . . ." Ibid., 387.

p. 138, "General Lee, I have no . . ." Edward J. Stackpole and Wilbur S. Nye, *The Battle of Gettysburg: A Guided Tour,* revised by Bradley M. Gottfried (Mechanicsburg, PA: Stackpole Books, 1998), 108.

p. 138, "The meeting was as . . ." D. A. Kinsley, *Custer: Favor the Bold: A Soldier's Story* (New York: Promontory Press, 1992), 151–152.

p. 138-139, "I never saw . . ." Taylor, *Duty Faithfully Performed,* 155.

p. 139, "Too bad! . . ." Ibid.

CHAPTER NINE: Retreat, Siege, and Surrender

p. 141, "it will be seen . . ." Gallagher, "Robert E. Lee," 1160.

p. 142, "Unless there is a change . . ." Taylor, *Duty Faithfully Performed,* 165.

p. 145, "With the aid of the . . ." Ulysses S. Grant, *Personal Memoirs of U. S. Grant* Vol. 2 (Scituate, MA: Digital Scanning, 1998), 115.

p. 146, "a wild and prolonged cheer . . ." Gallagher, "Robert E. Lee," 1161.

p. 147, "General Grant earned the title . . ." Walter H. Taylor, *General Lee: His Campaigns in Virginia, 1861–1865* (Lincoln: University of Nebraska Press, 1994), 233.

p. 148, "I had rather die . . ." Robert K. Krick, *The American Civil War: The war in the East 1863–May 1865,* Essential Histories series (Oxford, UK: Osprey Publishing, 2001), 49.

p. 148, "I can scarcely think . . ." Blount, *Robert E. Lee,* 141.

p. 148, "The warmest instincts . . ." Ibid.

p. 149, "intricate, zig-zagged lines . . ." Ibid., 51.

p. 149-150, "It was undoubtedly . . ." Ibid.

p. 149, "I have always . . ." Grant, *Personal Memoirs,* vol. 2, 276.

p. 150, "It was not war . . ." Ibid.

p. 150, "We must destroy. . ." Gallagher, "Robert E. Lee," 1162.

p. 151, "eat out Virginia clean and clear . . ." R. Ernest Dupuy and Trevor N. Dupuy, *The Encyclopedia of Military History,* rev. ed. (New York: Harper & Row, 1977), 895.

p. 151, "We must therefore . . ." Blount, *Robert E. Lee,* 144.

p. 152, "The negroes, under proper . . ." Taylor, *Duty Faithfully Performed,* 200.

p. 154, "My God! has the . . ." Thomas, *Robert E. Lee,* 358.

p. 154, "Then there is nothing left me . . ." Ibid., 362.

p. 154, "I turned about . . ." Taylor, *Duty Faithfully Performed,* 212.

p. 155, "Orderly! Orderly!" Thomas, *Robert E. Lee,* 365.

p. 156, "Men, we have fought . . ." Blount, *Robert E. Lee,* 147.

p. 156, "After four years of . . ." Ibid., 148.

p. 158, "I think it . . ." Taylor, *Duty Faithfully Performed,* 220.

p. 158, "impatient to make up . . ." Blount, *Robert E. Lee,* 154.

p. 158, "Mr. Humphreys! . . ." Ibid.

p. 159, "I hope that I am better . . ." Thomas, *Robert E. Lee,* 410.

p. 159, "Soon after 9 o'clock . . ." Ibid., 415.

Bibliography

Blount, Roy, Jr. *Robert E. Lee.* New York: Viking, 2003.

Brown, Robert R. *"And One Was a Soldier": The Spiritual Pilgrimage of Robert E. Lee.* Shippensburg, PA: White Mane Books, 1998.

Chamberlain, Joshua Lawrence. *Through Blood & Fire at Gettysburg: General Joshua Chamberlain and the 20th Maine.* Gettysburg: Stan Clark Military Books, 1994.

Connelly, Thomas L. *The Marble Man: Robert E. Lee and His Image in American Society.* Baton Rouge: Louisiana State University Press, 1978.

Dowdey, Clifford. *Lee.* Gettysburg: Stan Clark Military Books, 1991.

Dupuy, R. Ernest, and Trevor N. Dupuy. *The Encyclopedia of Military History.* Rev. ed. New York: Harper & Row, 1977.

Foote, Shelby. *The Civil War: A Narrative.* Vol. 7, *Gettysburg to the Draft Riots.* Alexandria, VA: Time-Life Books, 1999.

Freeman, Douglas Southall. *Lee's Lieutenants: A Study in Command.* New York: Scribner, 1998.

————. *Lee.* New York: Simon & Schuster, 1997.

Gallagher, Gary W. *Lee & His Army in Confederate History.* Chapel Hill: University of North Carolina Press, 2001.

————. Gallagher, Gary W. *The American Civil War: The war in the East 1861–May 1863.* Essential Histories series. Oxford, UK: Osprey Publishing, 2001.

Gragg, Rod, comp. and ed. *A Commitment to Valor: A Character Portrait of Robert E. Lee.* Nashville, TN: Rutledge Hill Press, 2001.

Grant, Ulysses S. *Personal Memoirs of U. S. Grant. Vols. 1 and 2.* Scituate, MA: Digital Scanning, 1998.

Heidler, David S., and Jeanne T. Heidler, eds. *Encyclopedia of the American Civil War: A Political, Social, and Military History*. New York: W. W. Norton, 2000.

Holton, Bil. *Leadership Lessons of Robert E. Lee*. New York: Gramercy Books, 1999.

Kinsley, D. A. *Custer: Favor the Bold: A Soldier's Story*. New York: Promontory Press, 1992.

Kohn, George Childs. *Dictionary of Historic Documents*. Rev. ed. New York: Facts On File, 2003.

Krick, Robert K. *The American Civil War: The war in the East 1863–May 1865*. Oxford, UK: Osprey Publishing, 2001.

Leckie, Robert. *The Wars of America. Vol. I*. Updated Edition. New York: HarperCollins, 1993.

Longstreet, James. *From Manassas to Appomattox: Memoirs of the Civil War in America*. Cambridge, MA: Da Capo Press, 1992.

McPherson, James M. *The Illustrated Battle Cry of Freedom: The Civil War Era*. New York: Oxford University Press, 2003.

Nagel, Paul C. *The Lees of Virginia: Seven Generations of an American Family*. New York: Oxford University Press, 1990.

Rosenbaum, Robert A., ed. *The Penguin Encyclopedia of American History*. New York: Penguin Reference, 2003.

Stackpole, Edward J., and Wilbur S. Nye. *The Battle of Gettysburg: A Guided Tour*. Mechanicsburg, PA: Stackpole Books, 1998.

Symonds, Craig L. *Gettysburg: A Battlefield Atlas*. Baltimore, MD: Nautical & Aviation Publishing, 1992.

Taylor, John M. *Duty Faithfully Performed: Robert E. Lee and His Critics*. Dulles, VA: Brassey's, 2000.

Taylor, Walter H. *General Lee: His Campaigns in Virginia, 1861–1865*. Lincoln: University of Nebraska Press, 1994.

Thomas, Emory M. *Bold Dragoon: The Life of J. E. B. Stuart*. Norman: University of Oklahoma Press, 1999.

————. *Robert E. Lee: A Biography*. New York: W. W. Norton, 1997.

Wilkins, J. Steven. *Call of Duty: The Sterling Nobility of Robert E. Lee*. Nashville, TN: Cumberland House Publishing, 1997.

Web sites

http://www.stratfordhall.org/
The official site of Lee's birthplace, now open to visitors.

http://www.nps.gov/arho/
The site for Arlington House, a National Parks memorial site.

http://miley.wlu.edu/LeePapers/
A sampling of Lee's papers online, held by Washington and Lee University.

http://www.army.mil/cmh-pg/books/AMH/AMH-08.htm
The United States Army's official history of the Mexican War.

http://www.lib.siu.edu/projects/usgrant/
A site maintained by Southern Illinois University and devoted to Ulysses S. Grant, Lee's great rival during the Civil War.

http://memory.loc.gov/ammem/cwphtml/cwphome.html
The Library of Congress holds thousands of Civil War pictures, many of which can be seen on this page.

Index